BASIC INSTRUCTIONS FOR THE
SHY
Disciple

BASIC INSTRUCTIONS FOR THE

JOHN R. SISEMORE

Tate Publishing & *Enterprises*

Basic Instructions for the Shy Disciple
Copyright © 2009 by John R. Sisemore. All rights reserved.

No part of this publication may be reproduced, stored in a retrieval system or transmitted in any way by any means, electronic, mechanical, photocopy, recording or otherwise without the prior permission of the author except as provided by USA copyright law.

Scripture quotations marked "NIV" are taken from the *Holy Bible, New International Version* ®, Copyright © 1973, 1978, 1984 by International Bible Society. Used by permission of Zondervan Publishing House. All rights reserved.

The opinions expressed by the author are not necessarily those of Tate Publishing, LLC.

Published by Tate Publishing & Enterprises, LLC
127 E. Trade Center Terrace | Mustang, Oklahoma 73064 USA
1.888.361.9473 | www.tatepublishing.com

Tate Publishing is committed to excellence in the publishing industry. The company reflects the philosophy established by the founders, based on Psalm 68:11,
"The Lord gave the word and great was the company of those who published it."

Book design copyright © 2009 by Tate Publishing, LLC. All rights reserved.
Cover design by Kandi Evans
Interior design by Joey Garrett

Published in the United States of America

ISBN: 978-1-60799-060-4
1. Religion / Christian Life / Inspirational
2. Religion / Christian Life / Devotional
09.05.04

Dedication

This book is dedicated to God and the family of God.

I am humbled to think that he would let me tell someone, about the hope I have in God and Jesus Christ.

I thank my wife and children who, through their faith and perseverance, have brought me to where I am today.

Contents

Foreword
9

Acknowledgment
11

Welcome
13

What Can We Do For You?
21

No Eye Has Seen
27

The Bible
31

She Couldn't Hear but She Listened Anyway
35

We're Never Alone
41

Does Anyone Know How Much They Are Loved?
51

He's That Poor Boy Who Lives Down the Street
61

What Do You Want From Me?
65

Helping a Few in the Right Direction
69

Love God
73

We Belong
81

Trust in Me
87

He Stood Up For Me
93

And One More Beggar Comes With a Request
97

When All Is Said
101

Saved For Later
107

Wise Words
111

My Wish For You
119

Foreword

I met John Sisemore when the army moved my family to Fort Leonard Wood, Missouri in 2002. John led an in-depth, Genesis to Revelation Bible study that met for three hours each week for about 36 weeks at a local church. My wife and I still point to that experience as a special time of spiritual growth and friendships forged.

John's former military service provided an instant bond between us, but it gradually paled in comparison to his demonstrated love for Christ. John served our country faithfully in uniform for many years. However, hearing John reveal his heart during our many long sessions in scripture, I was struck not by his impressive military service, but by his core love of our Savior. John taught me about servant-minded leadership modeled after Jesus, the greatest leader and servant of all.

John Sisemore would never agree to let me call him great. That's not his style and not where his heart is focused. His greatness is in his humility and servitude. Since "the first shall be last, and the last shall be first" (Matt. 20:16; Mark 8:34, 10:31) I look forward to rejoicing in John's reward someday. When I look at John I see a man who puts his faith into action, always acting for the glory of God rather than himself.

John's legacy may be something he will only see from the perspective of heaven, but if I know him at all it's not his reward he has in mind, but rather his love for Christ that drives his selfless service. I pray that as you read this book you are moved to maintain a lifelong relationship with our Lord. There's a life-changing difference between knowing *about* Jesus and *getting to know* Jesus.

Thamar A. Main

Acknowledgments

Pastor Max Lucado: I read all of your writings, some several times, and used them in Sunday school class on numerous occasions. Thanks for your stories that inspire.

Pastor Billy Graham: You exemplified Christ to me. Thank you.

Pastor Paul Catterton: You told me that we are all welcome at the table with Christ Jesus and were one of the first to make it real to me in every way.

Bob Knight: You lived what Jesus taught and gave of yourself so others could see Christ's love for them.

Pastor Greg Olsen: Someone who I trust with all that I have, for I have seen his love for Jesus.

Rusty Wilder: Who stood with me and prayed when I didn't have a job.

Thamar Main: Who is truly a brother in Christ.

Kenneth W. Bates: The guitar man who sang of the love of Jesus to all who would hear.

Pastor Eddie Gipson: One who read my stories and encouraged me to continue.

Welcome

God loves us more than we could ever imagine and loves to hear us speak to others about him. So if you feel that you can't talk about God to others then you need to read this passage: 1 Peter 3: 15, "But in your hearts set apart Christ as Lord. Always be prepared to give an answer to every one who asks you to give the reason for the hope that you have. But do this with gentleness and respect." This is where we start our walk with Christ Jesus being an example to all who will gather. I'm here to encourage you to talk to others about your hope, love, peace, and grace, which is given to us as our relationship grows with God.

Sometime ago, I got a job working one-on-one with high school students. The week before the fall semester began, I received a letter from the school district notifying teachers of their schedule. They were to report three days before classes began to set up their classrooms. So, I arrived that day with the teachers, willing to help wherever I could. Around noon one of the staff came to me and related that this time was for the teachers and I did not have to be at school. The extra time was so that the teachers could get their classrooms ready. I felt I wasn't welcome in a place I thought I belonged. It's like going to church and having the feeling that you are the outsider. I felt that way for many years and avoided going to church because of that feeling. I considered all of those who ignored me to be hypocrites who were only there to promote themselves. It wasn't really like that, but we do sometimes feel that we are not welcome in places where we want to be. We may not feel welcomed by those in church, but we know that we are there for Christ Jesus and we are always welcomed into the family of God. I stayed for most of the day and helped where I was asked to help. I hope that through these stories you will have a better understanding of what it's like to be loved by God. Thank you, Father, for the things you do for us everyday and we will continue to call others so they too know your love.

His name is Mike and his buddy was his Grandpa, who everyone called Howie. Howie loved to fish and had a nice boat he pulled behind his truck. Mike liked to go to Grandpa's sometimes just to sit in his boat and pretend he was fishing. Then again, Grandpa couldn't resist the idea of taking Mike, Mike's Dad, and his uncle fishing whenever they were all together. It was on one of those fishing trips that Mike may have had more influence upon his Dad and Grandpa than even he knew. They were fishing up on the Sound, just at the mouth of the Pacific Ocean, and they were getting some nice bites from the Salmon running into the Sound from the ocean. Then all of a sudden, Mike, who was about nine, started to reel his line in. His Dad just thought that Mike was getting tired of fishing and wanted to see if by chance he had something at the end of the fishing line. What he didn't know was that he did, and then all of a sudden the line became tight and started to go back out. You see, Mike had just hooked into a very large fish that was quite a ways from the boat. He looked at his Dad with that "I don't want to do this" face, and Dad just laughed a little harder. He had not told Grandpa yet, because if he did, Grandpa might get too excited and want to help. So Mike started to reel in the line and hold onto the pole that was cradled in a pole holder. He had to have reeled that line for what seemed ten minutes before Grandpa noticed what was going on. Yes, Grandpa got excited so much that he almost pushed Dad off the boat. He wanted to be as close to his grandson as a person could get. You could see on his face that all the experience Grandpa had in fishing was waiting for that little voice to say, "Okay Grandpa I think I need some help now." When Mike looked up at his Grandpa and said that he needed help, Grandpa was right there with his hand in his grandson's hand, helping him bring in the big one. Just like Mike and his Grandpa, we all have someone who gets as close to us as he can. He wants to help us in all that we do and waits for the moment to do so. All that we have to do is look up and ask for his help. He truly waits for us with love and kindness, sending those around him to help show us the path that leads to the Son, who lights the way. Our Lord and Savior Jesus Christ is the path home for all who ask. So now if you haven't asked it's never too late to ask Jesus to come into your heart. "Keep on loving each other as brothers. Do not forget to entertain strangers, for by so doing some people have entertained angels without knowing it" (Hebrews 13:1–2).

This is a story about how we are welcomed into the family of God. Here he comes with that big smile on his face. No one should be that happy. "Hi, my name is John, do I know you?" He said, "Yes, maybe you do, at least I hope you do. I've been talking to you since before you were born. You have read about me for many years. I gave you things to think about and things to do. Sometimes you were slow and sometimes you didn't understand, but you have tried to do the things our Father has asked."

What do you say to Jesus when he sits right next to you? I didn't say anything; I just sat there staring at him. He looked back at me with that big grin and said, "Okay what do you think?" I didn't know what to think. "Think about what?" I asked.

He said, "Think about what I want you to do." All that I could think about was he wanted me to do something, and I was thinking, *I'm not worthy*.

Oh my, it's easy to read the Bible and see what was written so long ago, but you can close your Bible and not think about it again until you want to. You can rationalize what you do, because everyone else does the same thing. But now you can't do that because he is sitting right next to you. He says he'll make it easy for me. I only have to give one simple answer. I said, "Answer? Answer what? I still don't know the question." Then I start to think about what he wants me to say and think about the Ten Commandments. After all, aren't they the basis for most religions, anyway? I want to know so many things—how he feels about what's going on in the churches, how to get back those who have strayed, how to bring more home to him. My mind goes back to the Ten Commandments and I say, "How about the Ten Commandments? Is that it, and do you want me to say them?" Then I think about the funny cartoon I have to remind me of them. He looks at me with a grin and says, "It's a good start, but remember I came down here before to help you understand what is really needed. Remember Exodus 20:13: "You shall not murder, but forsake yourself for someone, to lay down your life for another. To honor not just your Mother and Father, but also all of those who honor God."

It starts to make you cry, because if there is anything in this world I want to get right, it's this. I want Jesus with his great big smile to smile down on me. I want to show him that the sacrifices he made for us, because he loves us, are not in vain. I ask him a question about what he said in John chapter 21, when he asked Peter if Peter loved him, and how he wanted Peter to feed his sheep, to take the Gospel to others. His eyes got brighter and he said, "You are getting closer." He said "Now, what do you think is important? What could you give to others that would make them want to be with me?" Of course, I'm thinking, *Who wouldn't want to run around with Jesus?* but that wasn't the answer.

Then it hits me, that verse in the Bible that starts with loving God. How does that go? I want to get it right, not mess it up; after all, he's sitting right next to me. Then I find it. It's in Luke chapter ten, and it goes like this: "Love the Lord your God with all your heart and with all your soul and with all your strength and with all your mind, and love your neighbor as yourself." That has to be it, those two things Jesus said so long ago. So I look him in the face and say it to him. He now has a great big smile on his face. He says to me, "You have it, but there is one word that brings all of this closer to your heart. What do you think that is?" Then he said, "Let me give you a hint. It's said in church every Sunday and whenever someone comes to visit."

Now I have been sitting there next to Jesus for about thirty minutes, and in one word I am going to sum up what has been said for thousands of years. Yes, that would be a good thing to do. Jesus says again, "What do you think about your family and friends when they come to your house? What do you think about, or how do you feel when they come?" When I think about it, there is a warmth at home when the children all come back for a visit. We talk, eat, laugh, and reminisce about old friends and family members. We hug and touch each other's hearts. We look at the old movies and laugh at what we looked like back when. Then Jesus says, "When you come to my house, how do you feel? Don't you do the same things? Don't you laugh and don't you cry? Isn't it wonderful to be in a place where all things are possible? I sit here with you and listen to your stories. I see the hugs and the concerns you all have for one another. I'm happy that you came home, even if for only a short time."

He then smiled, and I knew what he wanted me to say. He wanted me to say the one word that makes it good to be here. He wanted me to say the one word that allows you to be yourself before God and in his presence. I won't let you wait anymore, because if you haven't figured it out yet, the word is *welcome*. Jesus welcomes us into his house every Sunday or anytime we want to. He's happy to see us, and when we talk to him, he listens and feels that welcome. So, welcome into the family of God.

So one day when you are sitting on the side of the

road and someone comes walking up to you with a big grin on his face, think about how he welcomes us into his house whenever we want to. Think about the love he has for us no matter what we do. Then thank him for visiting with you and giving you a little insight into what we should really be doing on this earth. Love God and love one another. Invite anyone and everyone to welcome Jesus into their hearts. He's here and he waits for us all, with that grin on his most wonderful face.

What can we do for you?

In church you may have heard things like, "By faith, and not works, are you accepted." You may have wondered how some people have been able to grow in Christ while others have not. Then you hear about the Book of Life and how if you really believe in God and Jesus your name will be written in that book. You see, he has done everything for us too, including giving his only begotten Son to die for our sins. Now I ask, "What can I or should I say we do for you?" Yes, I already know you are going to say that we are not going to get there by works alone. So what should we do to show God that we love him more than life itself? We help his children through difficulties, which could be nothing more than an embarrassment for you and me, but something extreme for them. Let us explore what can be done on this earth that would lead someone else to Christ Jesus. First, we pray for those who are in need of help, and it shouldn't matter what help they need. Then we need to ask for the forgiveness of others we have hurt in someway, and in saying that, I would like to clarify what I mean. If by some means or method I have hurt you, then let me be the first to say that I'm sorry. Those could be the hardest words you ever say to someone you have hurt. You could also say something like this, "Why have you done this to me, what did I do to you?" Someone has hurt you and you confront them with the "whys," asking, "How come you did that?" Let us start with the first one in that we all have hurt someone. What do we do to let them know that what you did was wrong and we really are sorry?

This is where that "What can I do?" starts, in that first you have to admit that you have done something wrong. On many occasions, I have done something and was never caught. Like the times between the ages of seven and nine when I stole food from that little store down the road. It was one of those mom and pop stores that had a little sandwich making counter. I would go to the store and steal bread, soup, catsup, and mayo on occasion. I would open the can of soup and eat it right out of the can. I would put the mayo or catsup on the bread and eat it as well. Don't laugh, I still have a catsup or mayo sandwich even today, but I did learn how to heat up the soup. I never took candy or sodas but only what I thought I needed to eat. I also remember that they would throw food away in the back of the school cafeteria, and I sometimes went there. It was wrong for me to steal the food, even though I thought I had to so I could survive. Now that I admit to stealing and even though the circumstances were beyond my control, it was still wrong.

This is where you come into the picture. We see others everyday who need our help, but we don't know what to do. Then I got this story from a friend that saw a man standing at a stoplight with a sign. It read that he needed help and needed money for food. My friend went to the local fast food restaurant and purchased something to eat and went back to the stop light. Gave the food to the man only to hear he didn't want the food, but the money. There however was a family sitting in the Wal-Mart parking lot in their older Ford Escort wagon. I assumed that Mom was in the store and Dad was sitting with the baby in the car. He had a sign, also asking for money for gas, so I asked where he was going. He was going to Bentonville, Arkansas, where his family was, but had run out of money. He said that if he could get enough money for a tank of gas he could get there with no trouble. He got that tank of gas and the eight dollars I had in my wallet. I don't know if he made it home with his family, but it doesn't seem to matter. It felt good for me to do something for someone else. It didn't matter that I will never know if his story was true of not. I did what I did because God told me that we are all his children and that we needed to love him and love one another. I didn't need to know if the story was true and if he was really going to Bentonville. All that I needed to know was that he was a child of God and he needed help.

There was one more time near Kansas City at one of those big truck stops where there are twenty or so gas pumps on one side and diesel pumps on the other. I was getting ready to fill up my gas tank when a man came by asking for money to fill up his gas tank. He got the last two dollars in my wallet, and I wonder why my wife doesn't give me money to carry. I know you all are wondering where I'm at so that you too can get a free fill up, but it doesn't always work that way. You see, I have this friend who, for some reason, is always around me.

I ask him for things all the time and there have been times when I got just what I asked for. So I ask, "What we can do for you?" Could it be a prayer, a handshake, a hug, or just someone to stand next to when times aren't so good? I have a friend like that and his name is Russell Wilder. We call him Rusty. He was staying with us just before he was to retire from the army. He had sent his wife and family home to Virginia to get settled back in their home, and he was finishing up some things here. I had been out of a regular job for about two months at the time and was subbing at the local school district. I also was teaching a class at an off-campus classroom for Drury University, but it wasn't a regular job. Rusty felt bad that I had not gotten a regular job as of yet, so in the driveway of the house he stopped me. He said we needed to pray for a regular job for me and he wouldn't take no for an answer. We prayed together and asked God to help me find a job. It made me feel better knowing that someone cared enough about me to pray with me. All the money in the world could not add up to what Rusty did that morning in the driveway. The next time you have the opportunity to pray for or with someone, do so. It will help them and you, and then as in my case, you will get a regular job.

My new job was in the special education classes at the local high school. Don't let them fool you, those young men and women know more about what is going on than we do. There were several people in the class, and they all had something special about them that only God could have given. There was Robby who was one of the kindest kids I knew and could bump heads with a bull and win. He wrote stories about monsters and they were very scary and complex. There was Zack who was in a wheel chair, but got to wherever he wanted to go. Sometimes he got into places he shouldn't have been, but he would sweet talk his way out of most everything. There was Jason who was deaf and mute and used that in many ways to get what he wanted. You see I got to be with all of them and especially Jason. I worked as his aide and went to classes with him and helped him understand what was going on in class. Not for one minute did I think that he didn't know what was going on. The girls all loved him and his cute looks, and he loved them all back with a smile and a twinkle in his eye. Then I got to work with Cory who was hard of hearing and lived to read about the Civil War.

I tell you this so that you know you can go just about anywhere you want and help others who need it. I grew up using sign language as my mother was deaf, so I was able to help not only the kids as their aide, but the families of all the kids. I got some of the teachers and students at the high school interested in sign language and started a class at the local church. I taught those classes for free for almost two years before we moved to another church, and I got another job with the government. So, take your gifts and talents and give them to others in as many places as you can. Remember that what you are doing is giving someone else the opportunity to give to another later on.

Accept all so that you too will be accepted. Then grab a glimpse of God's love and know that he waits for you to come home. Follow his example. Then show that to others through you actions—those kind, patient acts with no expectation of getting anything back. Some call it random acts of kindness, or pass it forward; let's see if we can't call it the love of Jesus. Thank you for coming into our hearts and leading us toward others, so that they will know your love for them.

NO EYE HAS SEEN

As a Christian, you may feel the love of Christ, but be uncertain about how to share that love with others. You may be one of those shy, quiet Christians who would be too embarrassed to stand up in a crowd to talk about anything, much less something you don't know much about. Start with what you do know. Think about where you learned about God and Jesus; was it from home or the church? Some of us went to church every Sunday with our parents, some didn't. We went to Sunday school, then junior high and high school Bible studies. Sometimes we paid attention, but mostly we played games. Some have never set foot in a church or read the Bible and may not know Jesus as the Son of God. They only know what has been told to them by others. So if you feel the love of Jesus in your heart, tell someone how that feels. Do you know what Jesus thought was the two most important things in life here on earth? In Matthew 22:37–40, Jesus replied, "Love the Lord your God with all your heart and with all your soul and with all your mind. This is the first and greatest commandment. And the second is like it: Love your neighbor as yourself. All the Law and the Prophets hang on these two commandments." I like to think of the Bible as "Basic Instructions Before Leaving Earth," an old gospel song I heard. It gives us the directions to follow as we learn more about what God wants us to share. Some instructions are not always definitive, but you can get through them with a little help from fellow disciples, family and friends. Where does that help come from? Consider your church. You do have a church, don't you? But then you may say, "I've been to church before, and the people there were rude and not considerate at all." Then find one where they are not rude or inconsiderate, but remember why you are there. You are there for God and Jesus Christ, not to make the people happy you came. So now that we have that out of the way, let's get started.

First, you have to find a place to do all that studying. Where could that be? Your local church is a place to start. Remember when you first went in and someone moved over so you could sit? The pastor that day said this is God's church, and everyone is welcome in God's church. After the service, you were introduced to the pastor by a friend or relative. You were asked if you would like to join a Sunday school class, because there are several and you can pick and choose. Then remember to be ready to give an answer if someone asks you about your hope in Jesus. Then remember 1 Peter 3:15 and the hope you have; you won't need to know Scripture to tell someone about what your love of Jesus means to you. Your first step in many to come: share your faith in God to anyone who asks. Share it with your family as much as you can. Start where you are comfortable and step out in faith. For a long time, I didn't understand what it meant to be in the presence of God. I knew he was there and that he listened to what I said, but I didn't feel his presence in my life. I heard about someone who would talk to God and get an answer right away. I thought, *How can I get that close to God? What can I do to show God my love for him?* I wanted that feeling others told me about. What I didn't know then is how much God loves for us to call on him. Because of his love for us, he comes running to hear what we have to say. One day, while driving in my car, I got the opportunity to hear from God and to know what others had told me about.

I was at a stop sign, thinking of my three children. As a parent, you want everything to go well for your children. You would move mountains for them if you could, but alas, you can't always do that, no matter how much you love them. So in my mind, the only one I could turn to was God. I told God how much I loved my children and asked for his help in watching over them. I thanked him for giving me such wonderful children, and I said he had done well in helping them grow up. I felt sad that I don't see them as much as I would like. I asked God to again watch over them, put his hand on them, and keep them safe.

Overwhelmed by emotion, I had to pull off of the road. I instantly knew God was there with me. I started to cry without know why I was doing it. Then I was told by God, *John, you know how much you love your family. I want to tell you that I love them more. I love you, too.* I couldn't control myself; I was shaking and crying at the same time. I felt him reassuring me, saying, "*I'll take care of them and watch them along with you.*" The peace that came over me was unlike anything I had ever felt before. I was humbled by the realization that God loves me enough to bring me such comfort and peace.

I now know that he loves us all that way. No one is denied his love, but some have not yet had the opportunity to witness it. He gave us the power to choose, and he waits for us to really ask. In Matthew 22:37–40, Jesus said, "Love the Lord your God with all your heart and with all your soul and with your entire mind. This is the first and greatest commandment. And the second is like it: 'Love your neighbor as yourself.' All the Law and the Prophets hang on these two commandments."

Now, even though this may be a hard thing for some to do, it can seem downright impossible for others. So, how do we accomplish this task that God has given us? We start with the ones we are comfortable with—our family and friends. Then we have to step out in faith, with the strength and grace given to us by God. Smile at someone. Shake the hand of a person who has ignored you, someone who would never expect it. Love and honor those around you—not only your family, but all those who belong to God, who need your hand to come closer to God , and who can see your heart as it is pressed against the heart of God.

Remember what you are doing. You're representing Christ and all those who have come before you. Remember the love God gives to you, which is unconditional. No one fails God when they love those around them as God does.

Again, how do you describe the love of God for us all? You don't; you give it freely to all who need the helping hand of God in their lives.

The Bible

"The Bible contains the mind of God, the state of man, the way of salvation, the doom of sinners, and the happiness of believers. Its doctrines are holy, its precepts are binding, and its decisions are immutable. Read it to believe, believe it to be saved, and practice it to be holy. It contains light to direct you, food to support you, comfort to cheer you. It is the traveler's guide, the pilgrim's staff, the pilot's compass, the soldier's sword, and the Christian's character. Here, paradise is restored, heaven is opened, and the gates of hell disclosed. Christ is its grand subject, our good its design, the glory of God its end. It should fill the memory, rule the heart, and guide the feet. Read it slowly, read it daily, and read it prayerfully. It is a mine of wealth, a paradise of glory, and a river of pleasure. It is given to you in life, it will be opened at the judgment, and it will be remembered forever. It involves the highest responsibility, it rewards the greatest labor, and it condemns anybody who trifles with its contents." There will be many stumbling blocks in your life. But with the help and understanding you receive from reading the Bible—slowly, daily, and prayerfully—you can use that to help others.

This brings me to another story about a man who all his life wanted to give to others. It seemed things got in the way and circumstances changed, which brought him in directions he had no control in changing. It appeared that all hope had gone, and people were starving in the streets. Bread lines were formed, and people were fed from New York to San Francisco. This man, who was barely sixteen, had to leave his home to work in a conservation camp. The pay wasn't much, but it helped feed his family who were but simple farmers in northwest Arkansas.

His name was Onia, and he was the first child of many in that family. He felt he had to bear the weight of his brothers and sister most of his life, because he was the oldest. He was fifteen when the depression was in full swing and was living with his family in a small area called Prairie Grove. They lived on the old civil war battle grounds, which is now a national park. He heard about the Civilian Conservation Corps (CCC) and wanted to join up. He lied about his age and told the recruiter he was sixteen so that he could get a job. He wasn't really far from home, just down the road in Devil's Den State Park, but in those days it could be a long time before you got home. He would try to come home as much as possible to help out. I remember him telling me about a dam he and his friends built in Northwest Arkansas, but I never put two and two together until one day when my family and I went to that state park and saw the dam. There was a plaque there with names cast to it. His name was on that plaque, and the dam was magnificent.

He said he learned a little about cooking when he was at the camp and would like to cook as much as possible.

He said he would always get a little extra when he did. He worked at that camp for what I imagined was about two years off and on. He really didn't talk a lot about it. He would ride his old mule wherever he went, and there are a few hills between Devil's Den and Prairie Grove, so it would take some time to get home. He was one of the kindest men I ever knew when he wasn't drinking alcohol. He told me that he wanted more than anything to be a doctor so that he could help people. He said that they had a doctor at the camp who helped a lot of the young men who came there. But yet again the alcohol became the stumbling block to him ever becoming a doctor. He attended church when he was made to and only if he was sober enough to go. But I can remember two times when he did.

Once was when my first Mom was alive, and we went to a First Assembly Church in Vallejo, California. He was dressed up in a blue-colored suit, which looked funny to me. He looked proud about something, and he was sober at the time. He talked to people, and they laughed and shook hands. It was like he was meant to be there in that place. The other time was at a church my Grandma went to in Placerville, California. It was shortly after my Mom died and I was living with my Grandparents.' He came up to see me I guess, and we went with Grandma to church. Again, he was wearing that blue-colored suit and looking proud. He greeted people he had apparently known for along time. It gave me a sense that being in church was a nice place to be. I still get that feeling when I go and feel the presence of God in that church, and it still holds dear to me. You may not have stumbling blocks like he did, but we all do have one or two.

So, when you gather with others, read the Bible and go to Sunday school. Start a Bible study class, and really study what God wants us to do. Then those stumbling blocks become less and less. Love those who may be a stumbling block for you, and with prayer maybe they will change. Use that to further your example of how the love of God transfers into the example you show to others.

My Bible was given to me because it would be appreciated and given to others. Wouldn't it be nice to have something to give to others, which would bring them the joy it has brought me? When I read the Bible I sometimes write down certain passages in my journal. Reading and using the examples given in the Bible can also bring you insight. It might not be a great revelation but a little feeling that keeps you from harm. That keeps you closer to the Father and gives you the strength to continue on, even in difficulties. God says in Proverbs 8:17, "I love those who love me, and those who seek me find me." I would like to say this brings many responsibilities, none which are too difficult. Jesus took the ultimate challenge and without a sound gave to us life everlasting.

SHE COULDN'T HEAR, BUT SHE LISTENED ANYWAY

What if you couldn't talk at all? How would you or could you get the message out? You can do many things to get your message across to others, which leads me to a story about my second mother. Let me give you a little background on how I grew up. My first mother and second mother did not teach me anything about Christ when I was growing up. My first mother died when I was seven years old, and two years later, my dad got married to my second mother. I don't like to use the word stepmother, because she really was my mother in all aspects of the word. She was born deaf and mute and through perseverance taught me another language. Then many years later she, through examples she got from reading her Bible taught me about how it is to love someone unconditionally; even her step son. I never really thought of her as someone who stepped in to raise me. She was there for me as much as any of the other people in my life at that time.

She was still very young and just home from school in Little Rock. You see, Lola is deaf, and she goes to a special school. She was home for the summer and was standing on the railroad tracks not far from her home in Johnson. She's mad because her brothers had left her. They were going to the river and didn't want to take her along.

Lola stands on the tracks and starts to walk towards the river. She thinks she can catch up with her brothers without them seeing her. It seems like she has been walking for hours, but she still can't see any trace of her brothers. It gets hot in northwest Arkansas in the summer, and it has got to be about noon right now. Lola decides to walk only to the river, but when she gets there, her brothers are nowhere in sight. She is still mad at them, but more lonely than mad. She starts back towards her house, and then sees a dog walking on the tracks next to this really old man with a cane. The old man is signing to the dog and at the same time trying to walk and hold himself up with that cane. It makes Lola laugh, that the old man would be signing to the dog, but then again, she does the same thing with her animals.

It doesn't take long for her to catch up to the old man and his dog. She signs to the old man who now has stopped and has a great big grin on his face. The old man said his name was Jesse, and he was following the tracks north towards Missouri. Jesse asked her what she was doing out on the tracks on such a hot day. She had almost forgotten what she was doing. She said she was looking for her brothers. They were going to the river to swim, but when she got there, they were gone. The old man asked her why it was so important to find her brothers. Won't she see them again at home? She said, "Yes, but I wanted to be with them. I and one other brother are deaf, and we go to school in Little Rock during school times. My brother who is deaf gets to go with the other brothers; why not me? I can do what they do, and some things I can do better than all of them. So why don't they let me go?" The old man laughed and said, "Because you are better than them, and I bet that if you asked your mom, she would say the same." It made her feel better, but she was still mad at them.

Jesse looked right at Lola and asked her what she thought was important to Jesus. She looked at him and said, "We all are important to Jesus, why would you ask a question like that?"

Jesse said that he was going north to check on someone who had been praying to God for help. It was important for him to help those who prayed to God for help or guidance. It, so to say, was his way of giving back a little to God, even though God has given him so much.

"Well, Lola, what do you think is important, and what should we be doing about it? I think that answering prayers is important to God and Jesus both. I believe they hear our prayers and come running to us to help us." Lola thought back to when she prayed and then realized that some of the things she asked for came true.

Jesse then said, "I see that some of those prayers of yours have been answered. So now what do you think you could do to help others who pray to God and Jesus?"

She had a great big smile on her face and said, "I could help them just like you. I could pay attention to what they pray about and ask God to help them, too. I could in some way help them with their prayer."

Jesse laughed and said, "Where would you want to start this helping others?"

She thought for a moment and then said, "With my brothers, so that they wouldn't be so mean to girls." Then she thought of her mom and dad and said, "I would like to help my family with their prayers first."

Jesse said, "You know, I think you're right about that. You should start with your family first. I couldn't have thought of a better place to start myself."

This made Lola very happy now, and she wanted to get home to see what she could do for her family. Then she asked Jesse how she was going to find out what they prayed for. He said, "It's simple. You just have to pray with them and see what they are asking for. Jesse said that it is important to God and Jesus both that we pray to them and ask them for the things we need. It's also important to help those around us when they need help. I'm going to give you an example of how I help others come closer to Jesus when I see them. I tell them how important they are to Jesus, because he died for them. He loved them so much that he gave up his life so that he could see them again. You see, that if you truly believe in our Lord and Savior Jesus Christ, he has said that he will see you again. What does that mean to you?"

Lola said that she wants everyone she knows to know Jesus so that she will get to see them all again someday. Maybe for the first time in her young life, she realizes how much she loves her family. She wants to go home now and be with them even more. She's no longer mad at her brothers and won't yell at them when she sees them again. Jesse then said, "Before you leave and go back to your house, say a prayer with me." Jesse starts the prayer with Jesus's name and then said, "Thank you for being here with us." The prayer went like this, "Jesus, thank you for today, and we appreciate what you do for us everyday. Today you have given me a new friend whose love I will carry with me for the rest of my days. Jesus, help us help you to guide others towards your light. The light that gives us freedom in knowing we are doing for others as you had said so long ago. Let us start with our families and continue on to others so that they all know your love for us. God, thank you for Lola, who in days to come will help those you have put in her path to grow in your name. Amen." When Lola looked up from the prayer, she was just a short distance from her home. She could see her mom waving at her to come in the house. She thought it strange that they had walked such a long way in such a short time. She then looked at the old man and said, "Thank you for talking to me on my way home. I hope to see you again someday, maybe even on these old train tracks." Jesse smiled and said he would see her again one day, don't you worry.

When Lola walked into the house, her brothers were already sitting at the kitchen table. They asked her where she went and why she was gone for so long. She told them about the old man and his dog and how funny he was when he signed to his dog. Her brother who is deaf looked at her and asked her if the man was deaf. She said she didn't know, but that he signed to her, so she just thought he was. They all wanted to know who this man was, and Lola said just an old man with a dog. Mom saw him standing next to me on the rail road tracks; she could describe him to them. Mom just looked kind of funny at Lola, and then turned back to the stove and what she was cooking. One of the boys asked her what this old man looked like, and Mom said he was just an old man and nothing more. Lola looked at her mother, and her mother looked back at her. Lola knew at that time her mother didn't see any old man standing or sitting next to her on those tracks. Later, mom told Lola that you can meet some of the nicest angels in almost any place you are. Lola then knew that she had walked with an angel that had come to let her know how much God and Jesus loved her and her family. She used that feeling and gave it to others all her life. Thank you, Father, for those angels and humans you put into our lives to help us along your path. Even though she couldn't hear it, it didn't stop Jesus from giving her a little insight into her feelings for her family. Just think—we all belong to that family, the family of God; and as you keep reading and studying the Bible, you will see just how close we are.

WE ARE NEVER ALONE

One question I had for many years was that I never felt good enough to speak about Jesus. I've done some regrettable things in my life from stealing food to survive, to throwing water balloons at some people in church, to expressing anger inappropriately. I would think about Jesus and wonder if he would want someone like me to talk about him to others. One day in adult Sunday school, a friend asked me, "Who do you think Jesus came here to save in the first place?" After that, I realized that my past could help others. After all, didn't Jesus run around with some guy named Peter? Peter wasn't always a nice guy; didn't he cut off someone's ear? What about the woman at the well? She wasn't a saint by any means; still, Jesus told her about himself and what he knew about her life. She had been married several times and was living with a man who didn't want to marry her. Despite her past, she went back to her village and proclaimed what Jesus had said to her, and they believed. Imagine what you have to say that would bring others to Christ and how wonderful it will be when you do. Sometimes the things you did before can be used to glorify God, because you're here now and because of his grace, you can relate to others your experiences and bring them closer to God. When I was fifteen, I got into trouble and was kicked out of the house. My dad gave me ten dollars and a paper bag with clothes in it. I made it to Bakersfield, California, with eleven cents in my pocket. With one dime in hand, I looked in the phone book, some how remembered my new sister in-laws' maiden name and called. I got her mother who came and got me and took me to my brothers' house.

This brings me to a story about Sam, who was only fifteen years old and kind of alone at the time he met this old beggar. He was fifteen years old, had a paper bag of clothes, and eleven cents in his pocket. He felt kind of lonely but mad at the same time. He was looking for his half brother that lived somewhere close by. He had been on a bus for about eight hours, stopping at every small town in the state. This story started a few days before when this young man was with some of his friends. They were stealing gas from cars in an apartment parking lot, which they should not have done. This young man knew that and stayed in the other car outside on the street. He went to sleep waiting for his friends and was awakened by the police. This young man named Sam had nothing to do with what the others were doing but was considered guilty through association. When the police took Sam home, his dad didn't care if Sam was right or wrong. He just wanted Sam gone. So he gave Sam a ten-dollar bill and a paper bag with some of Sam's clothes in it. Sam's dad suggested he live someplace else, maybe with one of his brothers. Sam left, not really knowing where he was going, but he got on that Greyhound bus early that morning. There was calm about him, but Sam didn't get excited much anymore.

So how does Sam find his brother, anyway? He got off the bus in Bakersfield and went to one of the phones in the bus station. He looked for his last name, but didn't see it in the phone book. Sam' brother had only been married a short time, and Sam only met his new sister-in-law a couple of times. He had to remember her maiden name and hope that the names in the phone book were the right ones. There were three names in the phone book, and Sam only had eleven cents, so he went outside. He was hungry and only had the change from the bus ticket. Sam went outside and asked some people on the street for money so he could use the pay phone. He was good at that, what they called pan handling, and it didn't take him long to get enough money for the phone and to get something to eat. Sam ordered a hamburger, fries, and a Coke from the cafeteria in the bus station and then went outside on the curb to eat.

Wouldn't you know it; an old man came up and sat right next to Sam. He didn't look too good or smell too good, either. It reminded Sam of the old hobos who slept under the overpass by the tracks where Sam lived, so Sam wasn't too concerned. Then the old guy just grabs a French fry and puts it in his mouth. Sam kind of laughed, thinking how brave this old man was. Sam looked at the old man and said, "If I give you some money, will you buy some food and not booze?" The old man said yes, and Sam gave him some money to get something to eat. The old man left, but came back in just a few minutes. He had a hamburger, fries, and a coke, just like Sam. He sat next to Sam, reached in his bag, got two fries out and put them in Sam's bag.

The old man put his hand out to Sam and said,

"People call me Jesus," and shook Sam's hand with a very strong grip.

"People call me Sam, nice to meet you, Jesus."

The old man had a grin on his face from ear to ear and kind of made Sam laugh. Here he was, over three hundred miles from home, eating a hamburger on the curb with a bum named Jesus. Jesus asked Sam where he was going. Sam said, "Nowhere right now, but I hope to find my half brother and live with him for a while." Sam looked at the old man and asked him what he did around here.

Jesus's face lit up and he said, "I work for my Father. I get to go everywhere and anywhere I want to, doing his work."

"Well, Jesus, what kind of work lets you travel like that?"

"I work for my Father and I make things new. I let people know how to contact the Father and bring him into their hearts." Sam felt kind of funny, not because of what Jesus was saying, but because Jesus's face really showed he meant what he said. Sam had only been in a church a few times in his fifteen years and had not read a Bible at all. These things Jesus was talking about were new to Sam, so he just let Jesus ramble on. Sam was half listening to Jesus and thinking about how he could get in contact with his brother.

Then Jesus said something that made Sam stop in mid-thought. The old man said, "Sam, when your mother died in bed at home, we took her right away to the Father. She's doing fine, and someday you will get to see her again."

How did this old man know my mom died in bed? When

Sam looked up again, there was a change in the old man. He appeared to be different, not in what he looked like, but in something else. A calm came over Sam he had not felt since his mom died. Sam looked at the old man and said, "Okay, who are you really?"

The old man replied, "My name is Jesus, but I have been called many names."

Sam could only think why would someone that important want anything to do with him? Sam didn't have a real bad life. Some of the places he lived may not have been the best, even some of the choices Sam made may not have been as good as they should, so why Sam. Sam just stared at the old man, not knowing what to say. Thinking this may be the last time he will see this old man anyway.

Then the old man started to talk. "It was a wonderful act of kindness you did for me, Sam." But Sam wasn't listening; he was wondering what to do. Then this old man said, "Sam, do you remember that time when you were nine years old and sick? You were staying with your brother and his real mother. You were in the living room lying on the floor in a sleeping bag and you had an upset stomach." Sam said yes. "And she said a prayer over you asking God to take away the pain. Yes, and the pain went away, but it also took the other pain away, didn't it?" Sam knew now who this old man really was. He hadn't thought of that incident for a long time. He remembered he felt lonely, because his brother had his real mother and his was gone. There was a pang of loneliness that only God could take away. That prayer did just that, and Sam could sleep without any trouble after that.

The old man said, "Sam, I knew that then, and this is

why I came again. You need a little help to get over this hump, and I'm good at pushing you over that hump.

"Sam, you and I have a special bond. You someday will do and say things that will bring people we all love that feeling of being welcomed into the house of our Lord God." Sam could only think how could he have people love Jesus and God? Then the old man started to tell Sam a story. He said it was in the Bible and very interesting. There were these people who didn't want to believe in God. They knew there was a God, but they didn't want to follow him. They wanted to do what they thought was fun and enjoyable. They forgot the laws God gave them and really didn't care. So God wanted to send someone to those people to set them straight. Wouldn't you know it, even the one God wanted to send didn't want to go. God told him where to go and he heard God say it, but he went the other way instead. This man argued with God, saying those people won't do what he says. So God put this man in the belly of a fish, and Sam was thinking, *This old man is really getting weird.* The old man said, "No, Sam, it's true, God put him in the belly of a big fish for three days. Then had the fish take him close to the town where the King of that area lived. God had the fish spit this man out onto the beach and then told the man to go and tell the people. Well, this man did exactly what God wanted him to do. He went to the king and told the king that God sent him and told the king he and his people had to repent. The old man asked Sam if he knew what to repent means. Sam didn't know and so he asked what it meant. The old man said it means to turn around. Stop what you are doing that is against the laws of God and start doing what is right in the eyes of God. You ask God to forgive you for what you were doing; ask for help to do what is right, then with love in your heart follow God. Sam was curious now as to what happened to the king and his people. The old man said the king heard the man and told all of the people to stop what they were doing. To change their ways and to follow the laws of God, they truly repented of their sins.

"So what happened to the man who told them?" asked Sam.

"You know, some people never learn. He was mad that they repented and argued with God again."

Sam had a sad look on his face and the old man asked why.

"I think you know why. I've done some pretty rotten things in my life."

"Sam, you may do some more pretty rotten things again in you lifetime."

Sam then looked at the old man and asked, "How can God forgive me for what I've done, or for what I may do later?"

He laughed out loud, and with a big grin on his face said, "Repent. The Father really does forgive and forget."

The old man looked at Sam and said, "Remember back to when your first mom was alive. What did you do to make her mad?"

"Many things, but once when I was five I ran away from school and went home. No one was home when I got there, but the phone rang and it was the school. I told them I was sick and my Mom was in the bathroom, I promised she would call when she got out. I never said anything to anyone, but hid in the closet in the boys' bedroom. The school called back, and when my Mom found out I wasn't at school well, let's just say it took a lot of people a long time to find me. Mom wasn't very happy and my Dad wanted to kill me.

"Yes, but what did your mom do later when she was on the couch? She had one of your sisters make you toast with butter and jelly. See, she still loves you and still wants you to have things you want and need. Our Father is the same way; he sees what you do and gives you the freedom to choose. He has given us the laws to follow and wants us to follow them. He loves us so much he is willing to let us choose, and he loves us so much he wants to forgive us. "Sam wants to know how that is going to save him, how God will forgive us and remember no more." The old man stops and again with that grin on his face says, "Repent. Our Father sent me here a long time ago to show you the way home. In many ways, I have done that very thing. To love and honor the Father is to love and honor each other. It becomes a natural thing to love others when your love of God is deep in your heart."

Sam had one more question to ask. All of this they talked about was still confusing to him. Sam looked at the old man and asked, "How do you love God?"

The old man smiled. "He's our Father and he created all things. He left us writings which we called the Bible, and it tells us what to do. But it also tells us how much he loves us. You can be told of his love for us and love him back, or you can read of his love for us. You have to choose what you want.

"So Sam, let the Father deep into your heart. Let his

love flow throughout your life. Then I'm going to ask you to do something for me."

Sam thought, *yeah, what can I do for this man who calls himself the Son of God?* The old man, with that smile on his face said, "Someday people are going to ask you about me and our Father. All that I want you to do is tell them about us, help them read the Bible, and welcome them to our house, the house of God."

This didn't really seem like a hard thing to do, but as time went by and Sam got older, he became much closer to God. It turned out to be a joy to tell people about Jesus and God. It gave Sam the opportunity to give back to God a small part of what God gave to him. Throughout the years, it has become what Sam is, giving to all who will listen to his stories about the old days and that old man on the curb. In parting their ways, that old man looked at Sam and said, "Try the first name of the three in the phone book. You might be surprised."

So I would like to invite you to come forward in God's house and let his love for you flow throughout your life and the lives of the ones you touch.

Father, we thank you for your son who came so long ago to show us the path which leads us home. We ask for your strength to keep us on the path and to bring more with us so we're never alone. Even though Sam was young, he had been through a lot and he saw something in that old man that brought out the best in him.

Does Anyone Know How Much They Are Loved?

I know that you may have thoughts about how you could tell people about Jesus. Don't worry, just start by talking to him yourself; the other things will come later. You may be thinking, *But what about the rules and regulations that come with all this stuff?* It seems like there are too many rules and regulations. People are always having meetings to develop programs to help people come closer to God. What happened to just talking to people about God and Jesus? Why are some people excluded from the process of knowing God and Jesus? You would think that if someone wanted to speak about God, people would be standing in line to help them. But lately, the planning for the program by the committee has gotten in the way. What do they call that—a stumbling block, which keeps you away from God? Sometimes it seems to be getting in the way of progress, stopping the growth, and trying to manage what is left. How do you deal with that?

You wait your turn; you don't stop the process because something or someone gets in the way. Eventually, there will come a time when you will be able to speak about God. Practice on your family and friends until that time arrives. Don't stop your reading and study of our Lord and Savior. Jesus came here to save us from ourselves. He was simple in nature and looked to those who needed him the most. He wanted all of us to know the Father, and he did not exclude anyone. Not the poor or the rich, the good or bad, and surely not those who thought they knew best. All of us were in his prayers to his Father, who loves us all. This brings me to the shy ones and to the ones who think they know what to do. Sometimes knowing the rules and regulations and following the heart of God are two different things. You get wrapped up in the ceremony and lose the ones you are trying to help. To those who are afraid of what is going on and don't want to rock the boat to speak, they just drift away. When people don't understand why we do things and are not given the understanding, they resist. Even the disciples would ask Jesus to explain what he had talked about. So what do you do? You open your heart first, then open your mind to how Jesus told his disciples. Be honest and look up what you don't know, just like you would do in Sunday school. "Does anyone know the spiritual condition of those who are around you, or do you even care? Let us not forget to be about the real business of Christians. Worshiping God, glorifying Christ Jesus, and loving one another in word and deed" (paraphrased from Pastor Candie Blankman in Downey, California).

So should we be about the business of Christians? Should we be bringing more and more to Christ? Using the example he himself used to bring us to God, let us examine ourselves first and be honest, even though it might hurt. I wanted to belong to the family of Christ. So I joined a church and I started to learn really what it means to love God. I saw others who emulated Christian love, and I wanted that too. So I worked on it, but I stumbled; Satan puts things in my path. He hates that my love for God and Christ grows stronger with each touch the Holy Spirit gives to my heart. Then I got to a point where I began to understand what that love meant to me. Unconditional, everlasting, and I wanted God and Jesus to be proud of me. Growing up, I didn't hear those words from my family here. Then it happened and deep in my heart, I'm told by God that he has always been proud of me. So I know my business is to love the ones he loves and to let the ones who want to know him love him as I do.

There are still stumbling blocks out there and I have one now even as I write this. The ones I'm told to respect because of their position in the church aren't always about the business of Christians. What do you do with them? You love them, you hope they realize what they are doing, and you pray. You don't stay and let them bring you down. You lift yourself up with the help of God. You start again where you see those who are truly Christian. If you think for one moment you are running away, you're not. You still have the love of God in your heart. You're just taking it to others who need it more. So move if you think the need is there. God will guide you to where he wants you to be. Go with the grace of God and be happy to serve him. It's like the story about the soldier after World War I. He was on his way home, but he had something to do first before he got on that ship home. He was in France when the war ended and was getting ready to get on a ship back to the United States. Then while looking through his duffel bag he saw that old tattered Bible he was given. When he saw it, it reminded him of the farm he had left. He had told his family that he would try to learn how to read it while he was away. He didn't have much time, but he would hold that Bible and pray to God to keep him safe. Well, now the war was over, and it was time for him to leave and go home to his family and the farm. He stood there on that dock in a city and country he did not know, and then realized he had to go to the promised land. The land where Jesus had walked and preached so long ago, he wanted to walk where Jesus had walked. He thought it would get him closer to Jesus, and he could talk with him better. So Edward left that city in France and started out on foot to the promised land. He was going to tell Jesus all the things he wanted to tell him all his life.

Well, there he was sitting alongside of the road. He had a little money, no food, and a canvas duffel bag. Even though it was a beautiful morning, he really didn't notice it. He wasn't thinking much about the weather or anything else. He really didn't have much in the way of material goods, but he wasn't sad, either. He was a farmer, then a soldier, and now going back to being a farmer, but he had a mission first. He had seen most of what he thought was the modern world at the time. He was going to the land of Canaan, somewhere south of where he was then. He wanted to see the places where Jesus had walked and had preached his sermons. He wanted to see the places Jesus had been and to walk in the footsteps of the Son of Man. He remembered stories told to him when he was a boy. He remembered stories about Jesus Christ, who walked on this earth and came to make things new. He never learned to read and write, because in those days farmers didn't need to know. They followed the seasons, knew when to plant and when to reap the harvest.

So here he sat when this young man came up to him. This young man had a sense of peace about him that the soldier could not describe. Then the young man pulled out some bread and a flask of water from his bag.

You know he offered the bread and water to me, no questions asked. The bread was good, and it seemed like the flask never got empty. He asked me where I was going, and so I told him about the Great War and how I had to fight in it. The war was over now, and I was going to the land of Canaan to walk where Jesus walked and to thank Jesus for saving me, not just in the war, but for saving me for all eternity. The way I figured it, was that if I could get close to where Jesus was, the better he could hear me. So anyway, I was telling this young man about how I left the farm when the war started and before I go back, I just wanted to thank Jesus for what he had done for me.

Then for some reason, this young man smiled at me. It was a smile like I had never seen before. He said he was sorry for not introducing himself when he first came up, and he still had that smile. You know, I felt a kindness and comfort in that smile I had not felt in a long time. Then he said, "I'm called by many names, but the one you used will be fine." You could have knocked me over with a feather. I know that he went to heaven almost two thousand years ago, but there he was, right next to me.

Then at the same time, I was thinking, *I'm not worthy to be here in his presence.* I really don't know what to do.

He began to talk and said, "You're welcome." I forgot what I was even there for and just shook my head. I realized he was saying you are welcome. It's funny how just one phrase can make up for so many things. He asked me what in the Bible what was the most important thing to me. I was kind of embarrassed and told him I can't read, but I do remember what people read to me and what they told me about him.

He said, "That's okay, but what do you think is important?" I thought about why I was even on this road and remembered that I came here to thank him. I looked at his smile and thought, *This has to be bigger than just thanks.* What should I say? Should I start with the Ten Commandments?

I had seen a lot of unfair and unjust things happen in that war. How cruel man can be to his fellow man. So now I want to know how Jesus would have handled those things. I looked at him and said, "I know you want me to give you an answer, but I have a few questions first, if you don't mind."

He gave me that smile again and started to speak. I sat there thinking how wonderful it was to hear the voice of God. He said he had many things he wanted to do here on earth when he was here before. He also knew he had a purpose for being here and that is what he did. He said, "Like you had a purpose for what you did in the war, only our battles were different."

The soldier said he remembered 1 John 3:16 and "that was when you gave up your life because you and God love us."

Jesus smiled and said "Yes, but what else? The soldier said that is why I'm here, to thank you for what you did. You didn't have to do that; you gave up your life for me and I wanted to say thank you. That's important to me and about the most important thing I know."

Then he smiled again and said, "Close, but not quite what I expected." So now I'm really in a mess. I have this old Bible with me, but can't read but a few words. It's been a long time since I sat in a church and heard the preacher. I was thinking, *why was Jesus here the first time?* He said out of the blue, "What do you think I came here for in the first place?"

I almost forgot who I was talking to and wondered how he knew what I was thinking. I smiled and said, "To help us get home. He came here to show us the way to heaven and to teach us that God loves us and wants us all to come home."

He said, "You're on the right track. Let me explain how much our Father loves us. You love your mom and dad, don't you? Your sister Ellen, even though she got on your nerves, you loved her more than life itself. Your older brother James, who passed when you were at war, you loved him as well." I wanted to cry, I had not thought of my family in a long time. I only got a couple of letters out to them. My buddies wrote them for me. He was right; I did love them more than life itself. The others in my family and friends, I love them, too. I got a lump in my throat and I could feel the tears on my cheeks. It had been so long ago, and I really wanted to go home.

Jesus looked at me with a smile and said, "Our Father loves us more." The feeling I got deep in my heart was almost too hard to bear. I knew then just how much God loves us. I was beginning to understand what was really important. Jesus said it before, a long time ago.

I said, "Jesus, what did you say to those guys who were with you at the Last Supper? You washed their feet, didn't you?"

"Yes, and I would do it again."

"You did that because you love them."

"Yes again, and I think you're getting closer to that answer."

It's getting really hard now, because if there is one thing in life you want to get right, it's this. You want Jesus who is sitting next to you to be proud of you. You want him to know that the sacrifices he made for you were not in vain. You want his unending, never tiring love to be showered on you. So you think about the love Peter had for Jesus. Then you think about that rooster crowing three times, and you wonder how Jesus could love any of us. You remember that part when Jesus asked Peter if he loved him. How Peter said yes and was upset about it. But you remember, Jesus still loved Peter and wanted Peter to spread the Gospel. You also remember that Peter loves Jesus more than life itself. That's it, Jesus want us to love one another. How can I say it and make it sound good? I wish I could remember that part of the Bible, I wish I could read.

Jesus said, "You have a Bible in that sack, don't you?" I said yes, but I only know a few of the words. He said, "Bring it out, and I'll help you."

So we turned to the Bible, Matthew 22:37–40. It said, "Love the Lord your God with all your heart and with all your soul and with all your mind. This is the first and greatest commandment. Then he said the second is like it: Love your neighbor as yourself. All the Law and the Prophets hang on these two commandments."

He asked me if I understood what that meant, and I said yes. "It means you love everyone, even those you may not like at the moment." He smiled. He said, "What could you do to help those people to love others?" I thought for a few minutes and said I could make them feel at home. Jesus said, "How do you feel when you're with your family and friends?" It's wonderful, especially during holidays. We sit around talking in the kitchen where people are fixing food; Mom has an old wood stove that heats up the whole house. We touch everyone with hugs and we hold the babies. We reminisce about ones who are gone and read letters and cards.

Jesus said, "When you come to my house, how do you feel? Don't you hug one another, talk to old friends, and hold the babies? I have sat here with you, listening to all the things you say and watching what you do. I'm happy that you come, even if only for a short while."

It makes me want to cry again that Jesus could love me that much. The simplest thing could make him happy. Then I realized that I don't have to worry anymore about what is unfair or unjust. I just need to love people like Jesus does. I know that will be hard to do, but I can start slow and build myself up. I can start with that stranger I don't know or with that neighbor I don't like very much.

What a peace I have knowing I can do something God wants me to do. I'll start right now. Then Jesus said, "I have something for you to do." A panic starts to crawl up my back. What could I do for Jesus that he can't do himself? I said yes, but I was really kind of afraid. Then with a smile on his face, he said, "If you feel the love of God in your heart, then go and love others. Welcome them into our family, the family of God. Bring as many as you can in remembrance of me. Then he walked with me for a while and guided me towards a town not too far away. He said I would meet some people there who were expecting me. He's gone now from my presence, but not from my heart. He will always be in my heart and I in his. So welcome into the family of God. It's so nice to see you here.

Most gracious Father, we thank you for today for your Son who brought us closer to your heart and for your abundant grace. As we go our ways this day, we will remember what you have done for us in Jesus' name.

HE IS THAT POOR BOY WHO LIVES DOWN THE STREET

So what do we do? Stop, find your purpose, and then move on with the grace of God. Everyone has something to give; volunteer your time to help others as Jesus said in remembrance of him. This brings me to another story about a young man who through no fault of his own was labeled. But just one person who knew him spoke up and things changed, so speak up for Jesus. You may be that one person who does.

I'm positive he's the one who stole the money. Haven't you seen him? He's that poor boy that lives about a mile west of the school. I know you've seen him; he's the one with the old clothes. It looks like he dresses himself. Where is his mother, anyway? Why, his teacher had to send him to the principal. They sent for someone to take him home to change his clothes. He must have worn the same clothes all week. How can anyone do that or let someone do that to that kid? Hi, Mrs. Moore, did they send that kid home from your classroom? What mother would let their kid come to school like that? The kid's name is Johnny, and he doesn't have a mother. His mother died the last day of school last June. It seems like there were different marriages, and all of his brothers and sisters are gone. His Dad works at the shipyard, and maybe he doesn't know what is happening. Johnny doesn't know what's wrong; he comes to school but keeps to himself. He had an older brother here last year, but who knows where he is at now. So instead of wondering what his parents are doing, why don't we do something to help Johnny? Johnny overheard what was being said; after all, they were just outside the door to the principal's office. Johnny just sat there, waiting for his dad to take him home. It's not known what happened to Johnny when he got home, but he was at school the next day. Mrs. Moore greeted him like always, and Johnny sat at his desk. There was, however, something nice for Johnny at the office. Someone brought clothes for him to take home. Johnny heard someone say it was the Christian thing to do. He didn't know what it meant until much later in life, but it never left his mind.

Was that a sad story or a story a new Christian could use to bring the understanding to someone new? Do you have some old story you could tell that would relate to this one? Then tell that one, too. Then do you have some old things you don't need anymore? Is there someone you know that would need help? Jesus said it several times, and I'm sure he meant it: love those who are his and do for them as he would do for you. Do you know another way to bring the love of God to someone else, even if they don't understand it yet? Is there a church yard sale or bake sale going on in the near future? Get involved, help out, and when someone asks why you do things like this, tell them it makes you feel good, because you're doing something to help others just like Jesus would. That may be the spark that ignites the flame, which brings Jesus to light for others.

What Do You Want From Me?

"You may be thinking, can I really be forgiven for past sins? How can I ask those I have offended, much less ask God, to forgive me? Let me tell you a little story about me that may reflect on how bad it can get and what you can do to rectify it.

"There are times in life when everything you have to offer is nothing compared to what you are asking to receive" (Max Lucado). By the grace of God go I, not by what I do or what I have to offer. How could you in any way offer to God what he already owns? Yet I still ask for things everyday. I pray to God for things for myself and for others. I want things to change or be the same, so I pray. I tell God that I know I have to forgive that person who has offended me and ask for the strength and courage to do so. Then I don't always do what I asked God to give me the strength to do. I am but human, and with those come things I don't understand. I want to do what God wants, but alas, I don't.

This brings me to something that took many years to resolve. I had treated someone with disrespect and hated what she had done. How angry I was at those times in my life, and how could anyone forgive me for what I did to her? Because she was the only one I could blame, I blamed her for all the bad things around me. Again I don't want to tell others how I survived growing up at this time. Instead of protecting my little sister, I let the circumstances around us continue and they were not good. Instead of teaching her what to do, I let her decide, and she was smaller than I. Oh you could say that I was just a child also, but even as a child, I should have protected her from at least some of the things that happened. I just let it go or encouraged it to happen without thinking of the results.

I was about sixteen when I first realized what I had done by not being there for her. We went to what I thought looked like a concentration camp somewhere in northern California. She had been incarcerated there for some time, for running away or drugs, who knows what it was. It, however, changed what I thought of her when I saw her walking out that front gate. She didn't look like herself. It was as if I was looking at someone I knew but couldn't recognize. I didn't know how to react to what I saw, so I kept quiet. I was unchurched, so since I didn't have anyone to turn to, I kept it to myself. What a waste of a life. How could I ever ask her to forgive me, when I did so much to hurt her? I thought, *But wait, didn't she hurt me, too? Didn't she cause me to get beat up? Wasn't it because of her I slept in the garages or on the porches of the many houses we lived in? Wasn't I right in not doing anything for her?* No, I was wrong, and I have to live with that for the rest of my life.

How can I ask for anything, when I have nothing to offer in return? God has the answer and it starts like this.

Repent. Do you really know what that means? It's the hardest thing in life you could ever do, but the rewards are so many, you could not count them in ten lifetimes. Turn around and stop what you are doing, then ask God not only to forgive what you have done, but acknowledge to yourself what you have done and try the best you can to do what is right. I told you it wouldn't be easy, didn't I? You will slip, stumble, and fall on many occasions, but then something happens. The slipping, stumbling, and falling become less and less. They never stop, just become less and less. And you learn that when you do stumble or fall, you have someone to call upon to help you. You have the one who loves you so much that he was willing to give his all just for you. He is the One who still today grants your every need, but saves your wishes for when you are with him in heaven. Then you will know.

Throughout my life, people have come and gone; only a few have remained close. Some have gone on before me to a better place and are waiting for the day I arrive. I want to be there with them, but I know that as long as I'm here, I want to bring others to the joy I have received from the love of God. So when you think that what you have done is too much to forgive, remember God loves you more than life itself. So tell someone how it feels to be loved by God. Show them by the example you live that no matter how bad it gets, they only have to ask for help. If God doesn't come down himself, he would surely put something in your path to lead you in the right direction. So many people want to help, they just haven't been asked. So take the love of God wherever you go and give a little of it back to others. Then help those people God has put in your path.

Then go to the one you have hurt the most and, with your heart wide open, ask for forgiveness. You might be surprised to hear those words you thought you could never hear. "I forgive you, I'm your sister or brother, and because God loves us all, we should love one another." That kind of forgiveness is one that will uplift you to new heights far beyond what you have felt before. Look for opportunities to share stories you have with the ones God puts in your path. Then thank our Father for all the things he does for us everyday. His forgiveness is forever.

So you see, you can and will be forgiven. Ask from your heart and don't let your pride get in the way of a loving relationship with those around you. Thank you, Father, for the forgiveness given and for your Son, who gave his all for us.

Helping a Few in the Right Direction

Hopefully you are moving in the right direction and starting to feel that you can make a difference in the life of someone else. Someone you love and want to see again many times. In 2 Peter 1:5–8, it talks about what you should do to help a few in the right direction.

I do nothing, for God does it all. I can't save you and I can't give you eternal life, but he can. So follow me, and we will both follow Jesus. Then when our journey is ended, friend, we too will see him. He'll have that smile on his face, the twinkle in his eye, and the love in his heart for us both. So if you have a friend you can't live without, take him or her by the hand. Walk together towards the one who loves you the most. As you walk towards his place in eternity, bring those you love with you, the ones who also want to see his face. Bring your fear, for he will be there to give you life again.

I write this not for me, and then again it is for me. I get to talk to God and Jesus everyday, as in 2 Peter 1:5–8: "For this very reason, make every effort to add to your faith goodness; and to goodness, knowledge; and to knowledge, self control; and to self control, perseverance; and to perseverance, Godliness; and to Godliness, brotherly kindness; and to brotherly kindness, love. For if you possess these qualities in increasing measure, they will keep you from being ineffective and unproductive in your knowledge of our Lord Jesus Christ."

I ran into a friend, who I knew was having some family problems. It had been several years since I had seen her or her family. In that time, her marriage had dissolved and her children had gone their own ways, with her son ending up in prison. It had been a difficult period, but she was finally getting back on her feet. She had heard that we left our old church and asked if we were going to another church. I told her about the new church and invited her to come and see. She looked surprised that I had invited her, and when I said she was really welcome to come to church, she related what happened at our old church. She had gone back and was greeted by several of the people who had been there a long time. She expected it would be different coming back to the church, but she didn't know how much. She was greeted by someone she knew from before, but when she mentioned where her son was, this proclaimed Christian stepped backwards. He then made an excuse to leave the area, basically running down the hall to speak with someone else. It was obvious this hurt her a lot, and I really didn't know what to say. I said, "I can't explain why this person would do that, but Jesus would never leave you and neither will I." I don't know where that came from, but I said it. I don't even know if she heard it, but I gave her a hug and again said she was welcome to come to church with us.

It was about one month later and we were getting boxes ready for our Angel Food distribution basket program. I was in line and putting different canned goods into a box when I saw her standing in line. I finished my box and walked over to her and gave her a hug. It made me feel good to welcome her, that tingling kind of good. She had a smile on her face and I said, "So now that you know where the church is, I hope to see you on Sunday." With great thanks to God and Jesus, she is now coming to church, bringing her husband and grandchild. She helps out with the children's Sunday school. Did I help someone go in the right direction, or was it Jesus giving her a little push in the right direction? He wants us all to come to him whenever or where ever we are.

Some of us have been on the other end of that kind of conversation, where people will be your friend at their convenience. Where others appear to have all the concern in the world, but then for some reason, when you need help they aren't anywhere to be seen. It is like having some kind of incurable disease and no one wants to be around you. As a young man, I lived in a rough neighborhood and had been excluded by *so-called* adults. I was asked on several occasions to leave their homes because I was not like them. It was okay to be nice to me in school, but for whatever reason, I wasn't always welcome in their homes. Thanks to God and Jesus and their teachings in the Bible, I know that I'm welcome in the house of God. I know that I'm a part of the family of God and will be welcomed when it is my time to go. What a wonderful feeling that will be.

When you get a chance to share the love of God to someone, make every effort to show the kindness of Jesus. Help them to understand what it means to be a Christian and follow the teachings of Christ. Then Jesus will do the rest.

LOVE GOD

I have been telling stories and giving examples of what you should do, but now I give you Scripture to show you what you can see. If you read these chapters and verses, it will show you a little about what was given so long ago. Use all things in the Bible to guide you to that better place, the one right next to the angel who is standing next to Jesus, excited about what you are doing in his name. Love God.

> "Hear, O Israel: The Lord our God, the Lord is one. Love the Lord your God with all your heart and with all your soul and with all your strength" (Deuteronomy 6:4–5).

> Let your goal be his goal, and then watch the smile on his face. He really loves you and me. What does God really want us to do? In listing these passages in the Bible and describing them as others have related them, maybe you can get the idea deep in your heart on how your goal really is his.

> Now there was a man of the Pharisees named Nicodemus, a member of the ruling council. He came to Jesus at night and said,

> "Rabbi, we know you are a teacher who has come from God. For no one could perform the miraculous signs you are doing if God were not with him."
>
> John 3:1–2

How would you relate that to a goal you might want to pursue? First, you would have to acknowledge who Jesus really is: the Son of God, the true Savior that came here to bring us home to heaven. His goal was to bring the words of God to his people. He came so that all may be saved, and he died on that cross doing just that. What should your goal be in this case? The same as his: let others know his words given to him from the Father.

In John 18:20, as the high priests questioned him about his disciples and his teachings, Jesus replied: "I have spoken openly to the world." I always taught in synagogues or at the temple, where all the Jews come together. I said nothing in secret. Don't let there be secrets in your church; all church matters should be open and on the table. This is not saying that people who seek guidance and want their problems kept quiet to protect others or themselves should not be up most in the minds of us all. Although when you ask about a church procedure or committee, you should never get, "Oh, that's confidential." If you want to come to a committee meeting or ceremony and are told you aren't a part of that committee or ceremony and aren't welcome, it might be the time to think about going someplace where you are welcomed. Look for a place you will want to call your home. Don't settle for something because someone else said it was good or because it is convenient. If you ask, he will answer you and help you find a church home you will be proud to tell others about.

"I urge you brothers, to watch out for those who cause divisions and put obstacles in your way that are contrary to the teachings you have learned. Keep away from them. For such people are not serving our Lord Christ, but their own appetites. By smooth talk and flattery, they deceive the minds of naïve people" (Romans 16:17–18). Have you seen them yet? You may not know them at first, but they occupy every church in some way or the other. You can't tell who they are at first, but they will reveal themselves to you in time. You may hear something like, "We don't know what to do with so-and-so. He or she is not doing what the pastor wants." You are new to the church, so you say nothing not to offend. This just encourages others to give you their advice about the others, the ones who question why some can and some cannot. They are stumbling blocks, and if at all possible, ignore or leave them to themselves.

Do not be misled: "Bad Company corrupts good character" (1 Corinthians 15:33–34). Come back to your senses as you ought and stop sinning, for there are some who are ignorant of God—I say this to your shame. Ever been around someone with questionable character? Then you did know me or someone like me. For many years, people avoided me and I never paid any attention to it. Only on occasion did I really notice someone avoid being around me. I must have really been bad company, but didn't even notice it. Not until I knew that God and Jesus through the Holy Spirit was deep in my heart, helping me along a path which would lead me to paradise. I was young at the time and full of myself. I wasn't bad and I didn't do bad things as I got older, but I didn't have that foundation you get when you ask Jesus to come into your heart. People believe that they will not be accepted by God because of what they have done in life. My pastor related just that to me after he had surgery. This leads me to a story told to me by my pastor. He related after having surgery and while recovering in the recovery room, he met a nurse. As one thing led to another, he told her he was a pastor. She said because of her lifestyle, her mother said she would be going to hell. The pastor asked her if she believed in Jesus, and would she want him to come into her life? She said yes, but it wasn't that easy. She had done some things that she felt were against what Jesus taught. He asked her if she really understood what repenting meant? She said to stop what you are doing or at least try to change and do what is right. He said, "Then in the name of Jesus, you are forgiven. She again said it can't be that easy, that she couldn't just be forgiven after asking to be. The pastor again asked, "Do you really believe in Jesus as the Son of God?" And she said yes. "Do you want to do what is right in the sight of God, or at least try to do what is right?" She again said yes, and he said, "In the name of Jesus, you are forgiven." She wanted to know which church he was the pastor in, and just then he was taken out of the recovery room. Will she be forgiven and come to know Jesus as her savior? Yes, sometimes that is all it takes—to know that you are loved by the one who created you, to change everything in your life.

"Unlike so many, we do not peddle the word of God for profit. On the contrary, in Christ we speak before God with sincerity, like men sent from God" (2 Corinthians

2:17). We all want to be acknowledged for some things we do, but do you really want to keep more than your fair share? I can think of several who have, and I won't mention their names. There are, however, some who need to be named, and one is Pastor Graham, who put God above all else and has shown us the entire example to follow. Did he make a lot of money as a pastor? Yes, he did, but you would never know it unless you saw all the programs that the money created. He was a true guardian of the truth by showing that you don't get to heaven by how much you make, but by the grace of God. There are others, but very few, because you see, we are human and greed can get to us all if our foundation is not on the rock. Think of what you need and use that as a guide. Then use what is left to help others, starting with your family and the church.

Galatians 5:1 shows freedom in Christ: "It is for freedom that Christ has set us free. Stand firm, then, and do not let yourselves be burdened again by a yoke of slavery." Doing good to all is in Galatians 6:2: "Carry each other's burdens and in this way you will fulfill the law of Christ." It's really awesome to think about those two verses, isn't it? God gave us the ability to choose what we want or to seek advice from others on how to handle a situation that comes about. People have a saying that freedom is not free, and that is true because you have to work at it. It doesn't come naturally and sometimes with that comes decisions that are not what God wants us to do. So when you think about that freedom in Christ, think about what he would do. Think about what you are doing and who it is for. Are the decisions you make for the glory of God or yourself? Are you doing things for your pleasure or to help yourself and others? The answer is truth and the truth in Christ that we should do for others. And you'll find that what you needed will come also in time. Do well to all, helping them along the way, and don't be surprised if he helps you as well.

"Remind the people to be subject to rulers and authorities, to be obedient, to be ready to do whatever is good, to slander no one, to be peaceable and considerate, and to show true humility toward all men" (Titus 3:1–2). Well, there's that do-good stuff again, but what if the people you have to work with are not good to you? Do you have to be nice to them, even though they are rude and inconsiderate? Yes, God has laws, and he put certain people in charge of those laws so they would be carried out. You say, "What laws, and who is in charge of those laws?" Let us start with the Ten Commandments; they were made and given to Moses to give to the people. This is a good start for anyone if you ever get a chance to read them. Then God put others in charge of the laws and churches throughout history. It really is up to us to see what is out there and rely on the word and works of others in doing what is right. We don't need to follow blindly those to say you must, but with prayer and petition follow the teachings of Christ Jesus.

"My brothers, as believers in our glorious Lord Jesus Christ, don't show favoritism" (James 2:1). It would be hard not to place your family before others, but for one thing. What is right in the sight of God? We really need to understand and read and look back at what Jesus did when he was here on this earth. His family was involved and on occasion followed Jesus where he went. At times, they did not and wondered why he was doing what he was. The one thing Jesus did not do was show favoritism. To him, it did not matter who you were, from the old man at the pool to the Pharisee who would seek Jesus' attention at night. He welcomed them all, and we also need to remember that. Something happened the other day that brought this to mind. I was called by a friend from a former church at the last minute to see if I wanted to provide a letter of encouragement or possibly attend a service for someone who had joined our former church after my wife and I had left. We left our old church not too long ago and have been attending another church. We have been involved in a Christian organization outside the church for several years. We attend services and meetings and retreats during the year to encourage more to come closer to God and Jesus. At these retreats, letters and your presence at certain functions are ways to encourage those attending the retreat. I say this for two reasons: we were not shunned or ignored by the ones from our old church. They are busy and it was nice of them to remember us, and if I was responsible, I may have called them when I realized the date for the retreat was coming up. Think like Christ, and do all that you can to not show favoritism to others. It will leave a lasting impression on those around you, because in the end, it is God's favor we want, anyway. You can't depend on someone else to do your bidding; choose yourself. Thank you, Father, for the strength to follow your example in calling all to your heart. We are filled with hope because of your love for us.

WE BELONG

Do we really belong to the family of God, or is this something people say to you so that you will follow them or God? There are so many examples and stories out there that I have seen, which bring all of this to a head. Yes, we do belong, and he wants us to ask so he can run and jump deep into your hearts. Yes, this brings me to another story, one where we all can realize the power we have when we pray to the one who wants to answer all of our prayers.

"If we live, we live to the Lord; and if we die, we die to the Lord. So whether we live or die, we belong to the Lord" (Romans 14:8).

What have I been saying all along? Yes, we belong to the Lord. We are a part of his family and we should act accordingly. We should have the gratitude and joy that comes from belonging to God. This is what you should do then to announce your life given to you from God.

Start with your friends and family tell them how it feels to hear the little whisper deep in your heart saying he is proud of you and waits for the day you sit with him at the table. He has prepared a place just for you, which is so special you will have to see it to believe it. You who think you are not worthy of anything God gives will get more than all of the others. For those who have given love will receive love from where it comes. Remember what Jesus said when he talked about helping those who need your help: go out and try it. You will feel maybe for the first time that wonderful gift of receiving as well.

My Grandma told me about those victory gardens and how they were used for food, but also to give a person time to be with God and to pray. This brings me to a story about a simpler time when most of the food you ate came from your own garden. They called them victory gardens, and they were planted and cared for by the whole family. It was World War II, and a lot of our young men were away in a far land, fighting for others. We did not know all the time what was going on, but listened to the radio and read the paper when it came out. They described what was going on in Europe and in the Pacific. Those were hard times for most, but they worked hard and gave what they could. There was a feeling of belonging to something greater than yourself. You wanted to help not only the ones from home, but the ones from all the homes across the country.

It started on a Sunday just after church in this small town, far away. His name was Johnny, and he heard what the preacher had said about belonging to God. It made Johnny feel good when the preacher said that. You see, Johnny's dad was away fighting in Europe. Johnny was only five and really didn't know where his dad was. Mom was working in a factory close to the house, and Johnny stayed with Grandma Fanny most of the day. Grandma Fanny had one of those gardens in her backyard. Johnny would help Grandma Fanny pull weeds and water the plants every morning when his mom dropped him off.

Those were good times for Johnny and he never wanted them to end, except he wanted his dad home. So he asked his grandma what he could do to have his whole family belong to God. The question was a surprise to Grandma, and she asked him why he was thinking that. Johnny said that he heard the preacher talking about belonging to God, and he thought that if the whole family belonged to God, everyone would be in the same place. He really wanted his dad to come home from that war in Europe.

Grandma Fanny, with a smile on her face, started to tell Johnny what the preacher meant about belonging to God. She said it starts in your heart and spreads from there. Johnny didn't know what that meant and asked if praying to God would start your heart. Grandma laughed and said, "Your heart is already started, but praying to God is the first step in belonging to him." She then asked Johnny why it was so important for the whole family to belong to God. Johnny said that if everyone belonged to God they would all be in the same place and that would bring his Dad home from the war. Grandma didn't realize until that moment how much Johnny missed his Dad. She knew they all missed him, but there was something special between Johnny and his dad. She then knew what to say to Johnny about belonging to God.

Grandma Fanny started by asking Johnny if he knew who Jesus Christ was. Johnny, with a smile on his face said, "Yes, Grandma that is God's son, just like I'm my Dad's son."

Grandma said, "And how much do you love your dad?" Johnny, with his hands spread wide apart said, "This much." Grandma said, "Jesus loves his dad just as much, and he also loves us that much. He loves us so much that he gave his own life up for us, just so we could all belong to his family."

Johnny still didn't quite understand what Grandma was saying and asked, "Is Jesus okay?"

Grandma said yes, and he is in heaven with his Father waiting for us to be with him. Johnny wanted to know what he could do so that everyone belonged to God. Grandma simply said, "You have to believe Jesus is the Son of God, we are the children of God, and that we need to pray to him and let him know you love him. Not that kind of love you have for your friends, but that love you have for your dad. The love that is so deep it hurts when you are not near your dad. The love that makes all things seems a little better and a love that is between you and God."

Johnny went to bed that night wondering where his father was and if he was okay. Then he remembered what Grandma Fanny said about the love of Jesus and God. So he started to pray, not an asking type prayer, but one telling God how much he loved his dad and that he loved Jesus the same way. It went sort of like this, "Dear God, thank you for giving us Jesus. You know how much he loves us, and I guess that you love us the same. God, thank you for my dad, because I love him like I love Jesus. I just found out how much that is when Grandma Fanny told me today. I don't know just where my dad is, but you do, and I know you love him like I do. So thank you for being God and having us be a part of your family, I guess that is what it is to belong, because I belong to my Dad. So thank you for all the things you do for us that belong. Amen."

Funny things happen when you pray, because a few days later, while working in Grandma's garden, Johnny looked up to see his Grandma hugging his dad. Johnny again thanked God for letting him belong and for bringing his dad home again. So when those days come and you don't think you belong to the family of God, remember Johnny and Grandma Fanny. Then give a prayer of thanks to God who gave his son to us so that we would belong to him.

Trust in Me

My hope is in Jesus, and I know that if you are reading this, yours is as well. I trust in him with all that I have. Have you ever heard those words before? *Trust me, and I'll help you out of this situation you're in.* But who can you trust? That's something very hard to do. You see, for most of your life you have been rejected. It will happen many times more in your life; you just haven't seen it yet. Until someone special, whom you have created a life with says, I know Jesus gives us hope. You hear them say, "I know who to trust, let me tell you about him, his name is Jesus." Some call him the Christ, the Son of God. He's the one to trust, because I have seen for myself what he can do.

Some will say, "Where are you going and why do you have to go? Can't we work this out, and is anyone going with you, even when you tell them they don't believe?" I say yes, my best friend is going with me, the one I married over thirty-eight years ago. You see, she is the one that showed me the hope I talked about before. She introduced me to this man they call Jesus. She helped me to understand that the trust you put in Jesus never fails, that he loves you more than anything else on this earth. You are very special to him, like a brother. So I trust in him who would lead me to greater and better things than I do now.

So we'll start our journey soon, with him at our side, knowing we can trust in him who leads us with love. As you go about your lives these days, remember he too loves you, so trust in Jesus. Then bring others to Jesus so they also know his love, peace, kindness, and grace. How many times have you seen those words or words like that in the Bible? This could be a good time to start looking through that Bible of yours. Look up how many times Jesus has said words like that or has shown him to be trustworthy.

I grew up in that church, the little one on the hill. I was not very trusting, which started when I was very young. I was just into my fifties when my youngest encouraged me to come. It was a nice enough place and the chapel—I didn't know it was called the sanctuary—was full with people talking to each other. I don't remember what the sermon was about, but one thing stood out from everything else. It was almost at the end of the service, and the pastor stood in the front of the people. He stated that it was time for the communion meal, and that in God's house, all were welcome to the table with Jesus. All were welcome at the table to give thanks for what Jesus had done for them. Don't get me wrong, but I had seen so much in my life. The words the pastor was saying were strange at best. I knew not everyone was welcomed in many places, but this time it was different. I didn't know where it came from, but something was pushing me towards that place where they knelt to pray. Then when I got there and knelt next to my loved ones, something changed. My apprehension about going to church in the first place was gone. It felt like I belonged there in that church, and those things somehow were not so bad.

You see, I as a child and young man was rejected by many, usually because of where I lived. I didn't have much, and that seemed to get in the way of others. It appeared that I didn't have enough money, influence, or my position in life wasn't what we want in our group or organization (church). So I rejected what they were doing, calling them hypocrites and other things which reflected my disdain for what happened in my life. Oh, don't get me wrong, I succeeded in whatever I did. Raised a family and contributed to his country, which I love. It was just that those who went to the churches seemed different. When I would go to a church, they would stay in their little groups. No one wanted to reach out to those who really needed the love of Jesus in their lives. Not until we came to that little church on the hill. There was that pastor, and he stood there in front of the church and declared the love of Jesus for all who wanted it.

We started classes to see what the Bible really was about and went to Sunday school. It was like I was being pulled towards something and it was good. So my wife and I continued on in that little church on the hill. We served the church and the people in the church, not for our glory, but for God's glory. I started to teach disciple classes and we worked together on a Sunday school class. Being involved with the youth of the church brought a great deal of healing. We worked on committees and attended meetings that were to help others in the church. It felt like a second family, a home where no matter what happened in life, you would always have a place you could come to for help.

That changed recently, and those who think that what they want and their status in the church is what is needed in the church have taken over. There are secrets in the church, and some are not welcome to attend meetings. They are for the chosen ones, and you don't need to know what the church is doing. They use the law to keep you in place and in the back of the bus, oh, excuse me, in the back of the church. They don't want you to say anything unless it is to do their bidding or glorify them. They parade in front of the church and say, "Look at me. I'm giving this much to the church and see how finely I'm dressed." The words are not there any more. The ones that said you are loved by God and that Jesus is here with you, that feeling of belonging to something, is gone. They changed the Lord's Prayer to something different and strange. The new pastor doesn't like children and has someone else do the moments with children. The new pastor only wants to read Scripture, preach, and occasionally sing to glorify the pastor. Others are accusing you of disrupting the church and not doing what the pastor wants. They lie about you to others and start rumors, putting the blame on you. We are having trouble in the church because of him or her. They don't question what is being said and continue the lies of others like nothing is happening. They are not like us, well, neither were the apostles. They followed Jesus and God and wanted all to have his mercies upon them.

It is hardly worth the effort when trying to explain away seven years, much less a life time. I thought why should I try to explain why someone who not only represents the church, but supposedly God, can do what they have done? So I won't bother anyone anymore with this;

I will turn to the one in whom I can trust. Remember him, his name is Jesus, and he loves me for who I am, not what I'm supposed to be. Trust in me, and I will help you with the burden you have. For I have loved you for all time and when you ask, truly ask, I will be there for you. Then turn back and love the ones who have hurt you. When you love them, they will see the example of Christ and eventually love you as well.

He Stood Up For Me

The other day we were discussing how our children had gone to college. The youngest is about to graduate and hopes to continue on to graduate school. Then it came to my son and how his first year of college wasn't what you would call scholarly. He, however, never quit but changed to another school, got his degree and certification and did this all on his own. My oldest child started at one college, but later transferred to another. She worked, had a son, and completed her studies for her degrees. I would like to say that it was because of me that they do these things, but I do think that they followed an example given to them by their mother. She supported them, stood up for them, and talks with them all several times during the week. She stands up for them and for me.

I bring up that, because it took me many years to see that the anger hid the truth. When I was a teen, no one ever stood up for me.

I have to apologize to everyone who has ever heard me say that no one ever stood up for me. I'm going to use several instances in which I know when, where, and who stood up for me. The first time was when I was seven, and I was sitting in a chair at the dining table. People were arguing over whether I was going to the funeral or not. I got to go, because someone stood up for me. I don't know who it was, but I have a funny feeling it's the same person who for years has been keeping an eye on me. I went to that funeral for my mother, God was there and he made the whole process pleasant. I at the time had four older brothers, and they were messing around in the back of where we were sitting. That only meant that I could have a little fun with them. It helped me get past what was going on, and deep inside my heart, he stood up for me and it wasn't bad, and somehow I knew she was in a better place.

The second time was when I was nine and I had gone to Modesto to stay with my half brother Danny. I had been down there only a few days and was getting ready for bed. I was sleeping in a sleeping bag on the floor in the living room. I told Danny's mom—her name is Opal—that I had a stomachache. She bent down and put her hand on my stomach and said a prayer. I never told her what happened, because I really didn't know it myself, but something happened. There he was again, standing up for me and helping me through something I didn't even understand. Oh, I had a stomachache, but I also had something else. I looked at Opal as a mother figure because she is Danny's mom. She took the time to say a prayer for me to someone she knew would stand up for me. He not only took away the stomachache, but he came to care for me as well. I no longer had sleepless nights as before, when I would think about my mother. I no longer had that empty feeling inside, because he filled it up with his love for me and you. He stood up for me.

Then one more time he stood up for me, and it was

when I was fifteen. I again got into some trouble with some friends. They were stealing gas, and we all got taken to the police station for it. When I arrived home at two o'clock a.m., my dad was waiting for me. He had a ten-dollar bill and a paper bag with some of my clothes in it. He suggested that I find another place to live for a while and said that my brother Danny might take me in. Danny lived in a little town called Oil Dale, just north of Bakersfield. So the police officer that took me home gave me a ride to the bus station. I waited there until I got the bus to Bakersfield. When I got to Bakersfield, I had eleven cents in my pocket and at that time just enough to make a phone call. I looked in the phone book for my brother's phone number, but it wasn't there. He had been married for a short time to a young girl named Lou Ann, but for the life of me I couldn't remember her last name. I had only met her once or twice before and at fifteen, who would remember a last name? So I looked in that phone book from the front to the back. Then it hit me and there he was again, standing up for me. I remembered her last name and looked it up in the phone book. There were three listed and I called the first one. When I called, this woman answered and I asked if she was the mother of Lou Ann who married my brother. She said yes, and I told her where I was and that I needed to contact my brother. She came and got me from that bus station and took me to their house. Again, he stood up for me; he made sure I was safe. At the end of that summer, my dad called my brother and was telling him that he was coming down that way to see him. I asked Danny to ask Dad if I could stay and ride home with him. After Danny hung up, he looked at me and said it might be better if I take the bus back home. Shortly after that, I was on a Greyhound bus going north on Highway 99, and I saw my Dad going south on Highway 99. I knew then that I would not be like my dad, but that I would do better than he did. Somehow I knew I had someone who was standing up for me; I just didn't know it for sure until later.

Throughout my life, God has stood up for me, always proud of me in what I had done in life. I know that others have stood up for me: my family, my sister Shirley, and all of my brothers. I would stand up for them in a second, because I know I have someone to stand next to. So when you get that feeling that no one cares about what or who you are, remember he does and he will stand up for you when the time comes. Remember your family as well, for they love you first just as God does.

Thank you for all the things you do for all of us undeserving people everyday.

And One More Beggar Comes With a Request

You and I are no better than the criminal on the cross next to the one who saves us all. That is what he wants to do. He wants us all to come to him. He wants to save us all, and he gave his all for that reason. It's hard to hold back the tears, not of sorrow, but of joy. If you don't know now, you will later. Someone, this someone, this man who is a God, gave up his life for you and me. Think about how much pain he had to suffer to bring one more home. I don't ask for me, but I ask for him. Think of those who you know. Think of those you will want to see again. Then no matter how hard it is, bring them to Christ Jesus. It can't be as hard as what he went through. He who saved you thanks you for helping someone else.

Remember me when you come into your kingdom, and he will say, "Today you will be with me in paradise."

How could we here today achieve what the criminal on the cross achieved? It's hard for some to understand, but if you really sit and read what the Bible says, maybe it's not so hard. What does God want us to do? Follow his Son's example, the one set on the cross. He not only suffered untold injuries but the ridicule of those around him. They laughed at him and called him many names, but he did not ask his Father to do anything but forgive them, for they do not know what they do.

I said you should follow what it says in the Bible, but should you follow blindly because someone said so? No, you really have to read those passages yourself, and then sit down with someone you trust and discuss what you read. In Matthew 22:37–40, he tells us to love God and to love one another, but do we really know the context of this? Then we think what about the ones we have hurt, or the ones who have hurt us. What do we do to love someone who we believe will lie to keep themselves in a position of trust? Then what do you do if the ones you seek to help with the situation don't respond?

Throughout your life, things will happen that make you mad. What you do with that anger is what this is about. The criminal on the cross next to Jesus knew he was wrong. He knew what he had done and realized that he had no power to change what had happened. That is, until he saw Jesus next to him. He realized the goodness he saw and the power it brought to this man and the others nailed to that cross. He knew at that instant when he heard others berate Jesus that Jesus did nothing to them. He changed in an instant because of who he was next to, and today he stands with Jesus in paradise.

We have the same opportunity as that criminal on the cross and we actually have more time to do what he did. We need to get closer to Jesus as fast as we can, because we don't know when we will see him next to us again. Yes, I said you won't know when he is standing right next to you. So by now if you haven't started reading your Bible or joined a group of friends to discuss what you read, get started. You'll be surprised to see just how close Jesus comes to you on a daily basis. I see things around me and in my heart everyday that brings me closer to him. Let's start with his power to change what has been set forth. So, you say things can't be changed or that you can't be changed? The criminal on the cross next to Jesus was changed in an instant. You, too, will be changed when you come to Christ with your heart in hand I recently have been asking for something for someone else. No, if you don't ask, he won't answer. I want this thing to happen, and in a way it is selfish of me to ask, but I ask anyway. I even get frustrated—or should I say angry—when it doesn't happen soon enough. I, however, don't think that my anger will get what I want done. I love God and Jesus Christ and will do whatever is presented to me, and through faith and hope, which he gives to me freely, I wait. I don't like to wait, but I do, because he said ask and you shall receive. On the cross after being beaten by men who cared less for him and then being nailed to a cross, he answered a request (prayer). He didn't let that child he created die on that other cross; he granted him his request and took him with him to paradise. A small request from someone with little faith, but still, a request asked of him from a child of God who believed in mercy. So I give my request to him who can grant that request, because I don't have the ability to change what I want.

I guess what I'm getting at is this: come to God with your requests or prayers as much as you want. Give them to him and he will answer them one by one, then with faith and hope realize he answers them with the love he has for us all. So I wait for an answer to my prayer, and I will accept the answer I get as I know it is good and just, because it comes from he who loves me. Then one more beggar will be again in paradise with him who would rather die than to leave us behind. Amen.

When All Is Said

At the end of the day, will those around you allow you the freedom to practice your beliefs, which includes the spreading of the good news about Jesus Christ? Then look around you and tell those you see how wonderful Christ Jesus is, for he loves them also.

Would you have trusted in God if you knew all things? If you knew what he has done for you, would you want to help others? Would you be thankful for the things he has done for you? Look at these three sentences from an article I saw on Gospelcom.net. Could you answer any or all of these three questions?

Let's start with the first one: would you trust in God if you knew all things? Most people would not. However, there are still some people out there who would. They are the ones who have had the opportunity to be with God through the Holy Spirit. They would not change anything which has happened or is going to happen. They know that God does what he does because he loves us. There is example after example every day of our lives. When you get up in the morning and you have already decided what you are going to do that day, God had planned this day before you were born, and it will go as planned, for he loves you so.

Would you really want to help others? Most would say yes but haven't a clue how to start. Start with the Bible and work from there. No one will ever understand the whole concept of the Bible until we have the opportunity to be with Christ. That should not stop us from starting our journey should it? I would like to start with the prayer that Jesus taught his disciples.

Did you know that in some churches they don't say the Lord's Prayer, and there are adults who have been in church for years who don't know it? *Our Father:* Yes, he is, and isn't it wonderful? Thank you for being at my side wherever and whenever I need you.

Who art in heaven: A place we aspire to see when the time has come for us to leave this earth. We will be with you and our Lord Jesus Christ, sitting at your throne, listening to all the stories of old.

Hallowed be thy name: How do I honor you? By giving of myself to those who need to know you. They, too, will have the opportunity to speak your name to others.

Thy kingdom come: Even though we don't know the day or the hour, we wait with hope to see your kingdom in all its glory and to be a part of your kingdom.

Thy will be done: It gives me great pleasure to do as you ask. I hope that I can impart some of the closeness I have for you on others. This way, they too will know that what you want is really what we need. Then they too can show others your will for us.

On Earth as it is in heaven: People say that if you look deep into your heart, you can see a little bit of heaven here on earth. I think that if you look around you, there are a lot of things which he made that will show you what heaven will be like. There are people here on earth who emulate what Christ has done. Look for them and listen to what they have to say. You will feel a little part of heaven here on earth.

Give us this day our daily bread: You have always provided for us, from the deserts of Israel to the fields of Iowa. As humans, we think that we do those things on our own. Those of us who have caught a glimpse of what you do know how you care for us in so many ways and provide for us everyday.

Forgive us our trespasses: We forget what you have done for us and continue to do what is wrong in your eyes. We continually downplay the laws you have set before us to justify what we do. Yet you continue to forgive us and remember no more what we had done. Why? Because you love us more than we could ever imagine.

As we forgive those who trespass against us: As humans I have found this a very difficult thing to do. We see harm done to others, yet we don't do what is right in your eyes. We think if someone hurts us or our family and friends, then it's okay to hold it against them. We wait for the one who did the wrong to reconcile before we forgive them. Start forgiving them no matter what they did, or if they ever reconcile. To forgive is what is important. Holding a grudge is harmful to you and them.

Lead us not into temptation: We can do that on our own very well, thank you. We need your ever-present efforts to keep us out of the mess. Show others through the Bible how God wants us to live. Then pray with them to lead a better, more productive life for Christ Jesus. It is our responsibility to help those who fall to temptation stand again in the name of our Lord God.

Deliver us from evil: He stands and waits for an opportunity to lead us from God. Don't let him; pray for God to intercede and he will. When you feel the presence of the evil one, stop and pray. He hates it when we pray and will leave us alone. I really believe that it gives pleasure to God to see that we as his children ask him to protect us from the one who would turn us away from him.

For yours is the kingdom: You who created us in your image have built us a place where we may come home to. The Kingdom you built and are continuing to build, which you give freely to us even though we don't deserve it. Thank you, Father, for your kingdom a place we may call home.

The power: All is yours my God, all power, all might, and without that, we would not exist. For your power comes from the love you have for those who you have created. Again, we thank you for all these things that through your power we receive.

And the glory, forever: May all the glory be given to you. We should acknowledge this to others, saying, "Glory be to the Father." For without him in our lives, there would not be any glory. For his love for us is what gives us the glory, which we should give again to others, for they too will know the love of God in their lives.

Last but not least, would you be thankful for the things God had done for you? Think about what you have, not in material things, but in the love of a spouse or a friend. The way the community gathers together to praise and worship God the Father. Are you thankful for those people who are put in your life to help and guide you? Then thank our Father for giving us so much every day and in every way. We surely don't deserve what you have planned for us, but we humbly accept what you give. Thank you for the blessings you give us every day, and give us the strength to give to others as you have given to us. Thank you for your love, peace, and abundant grace. Amen.

Saved for Later

He was only seven when his dad came to his school on the last day before summer. His dad had to tell him his mom was gone. Johnny and his brother Danny were standing in what appeared to be a supply closet next to the school office. Dad said Mom went to heaven to be with Jesus. She would get to see all the angels and she would be happy. It was hard to understand exactly what Dad was talking about, because at seven years old, you don't always know what to expect. There is a lot of confusion going on and a lot of people running in and out of the house. They seem to think they know what they are doing and what is best for you. There were arguments about who or if this young man was going to the funeral or not. Some said he was too young to understand and would be better if he stayed home. He never knew who grabbed him and put him in the car to go to the funeral, but he didn't care.

At the funeral, the family sat in an area away from the rest of the people at the funeral home. There were other people there, and they were walking up to the casket and looking in. Some were crying and would reach their hands into the casket and touch her. That little boy just sat next to his sister, quietly kicking his feet back and forth. Then it came time to walk up to the casket, and he was too short to look in but someone grabbed him. Whoever it was held him up so that he could see his mom, and then he touched her one more time. It was then when things started to change. He felt a calm come over him, and he could hear laughter coming from where his brothers were. Being seven only encouraged him to get down and play with his brothers. It was a distraction that came just at the right time, one that kept things in perspective. It wasn't a time of sorrow, but a time of happiness, one where there was laughter and joy. The way it should be, because when you get to go to heaven, it will be wonderful. So the funeral of his mom was not traumatic, but one of joy and playing with his brothers.

I think this is where Jesus came into the picture. Through the chaos came a sense of calm over all who were there at the funeral. This little boy, who would not know until much later, was being cared for by someone very special. Jesus said, "Bring the children unto me." In this case, Jesus came to the child. He was there to protect this child for something special. This young man's purpose may only be for a short time, or for only one person. Jesus knew the plan and purpose for this child and was there to help in every way he could.

Well, the journey has been a long one, filled with many hurts and just as many joys. Let me tell you about this special person that Jesus saved for later. He grew up in many different places with others who became close to him. He was angry at what he had to endure and as a young man and didn't think about the others around him. He got into trouble and ran around with the wrong crowd. But deep down, this young man was not a bad person, just a person who because he didn't know better made some bad choices. There's that choice thing, and you really do have a choice given to you by the Father. It is true, the only answer is that God and Jesus so loved this young man that they sent the Holy Spirit to him to help him along the way. They put people in his way to show him what to do. Like the policeman named Mike Sullivan, who was about to take him to juvenile detention, but thought this young man might make it after all and released him to go home. God put him in places and positions that would make him understand the love God has for him. God walked beside him in times of danger so all the others could see.

Then God gave this young man a friend to be with who was special just like him, but better. She would know what to do in a time of need, and he could depend on her throughout his life. God gave them children to listen to his old stories, laugh, and be proud of what he had done. They were children who ask things of their parents that were asked of God's son. Do you love me unconditionally? Will you love me even when I do something wrong? Oh how proud they are of their children.

God put people in his path to show him that anger gets you nowhere. He put people with whom he shared a past or common factor next to him. God put obstacles in his way to guide him to this spot. But the man didn't always understand. Just like a seven-year-old, adults don't understand all things. God knows that and puts people into situations to help them grow, to put them back on track.

God provides guidance through his word, gently moving them closer to his purpose.

There are stumbling blocks on the way and at times

seem tremendous. One is the feeling of not being welcomed. Most of us have felt that pain of not being welcomed into someone's home. It's not pleasant, nor is it a reason to stop what you are doing. Keep going and you will be welcomed, welcomed into the home of God. This young man is now an older but wiser man. He knows he has been accepted into the family of God, and he prays and talks to God almost all the time. It's more of a Father-child relationship that over the past several years has become very close. He talks to God and tries to do what is right to glorify God in every way.

So now he sits at the back of the chapel, doesn't say much, but what he had to say comes from God. You can see it on his face and in the example he sets for others. At one of those moments while sitting in the back of the chapel, he heard his name whispered. It was just a whisper and he looked around to see who said it. No one was there. He felt kind of funny, but he knew he heard his name, so he sat and waited to hear it again. He heard the whisper of his name, but also saw where it came from. He must have fallen asleep, because next to him was this man. Where did he come from and what did he want? He didn't look familiar and sat next to the old man and said, "Hi, do you remember me? I was the young man at your mom's funeral who gave you a hand up so you could see her. I was one of the other kids in that car with you when you had an accident. You see God is with you all the time and will protect you when you ask.

Father, as we stand before you, we want your love for us to last the eternity. We give of ourselves to you so your will be done. We thank you for your Son who took away our sin and showing us the path to your house.

Wise Words

These words were found on the office wall of Mother Teresa:

People are often unreasonable, illogical and self-centered; *forgive them anyway.*

If you are kind, people may accuse you of selfish, ulterior motives; *be kind anyway.*

If you are successful, you will win some false friends and some true enemies; *succeed anyway.*

If you're honest and frank, people may cheat you; *be honest and frank anyway.*

What you spend years building, someone could destroy overnight; *build anyway.*

If you find serenity and happiness, they may be jealous; *be happy anyway.*

The good you do today, people will often forget tomorrow; *do good anyway.*

Give the world the best you have and it may never be enough; *give the world the best you've got anyway.*

You see, in the final analysis, it is between you and God; it was never between you and them, anyway.

How can you explain those sentences to someone who doesn't know God? Well, let us see how we can. You see, you will develop friendships throughout your life. Some will only last a short time, but others will last an eternity. I have worked hard all my life so that I could be seen as a productive person contributing to the community. I just didn't know what that thing was until I met Mr. Kenneth W. Bates, who worked as an aide in the special education class at school. I was working as an aide to various students in a high school. I had been there for about three years at that time. Then this younger man came to the school to help in the special education classes. I liked him at first glance, and it lifted my heart to see him. Remember in the Bible where it is said that God will put people in your path to help you along the way? I had only been a Christian for a short period of time and was still learning about what it meant to be a Christian. Well, Mr. Kenneth W. Bates was that person God put in my path to help me along the way. It was like having a little brother again whom I could count on whenever I needed someone. Even though I didn't ask him, I knew in my heart I could ask of him anything. I immediately knew how he felt about God and Jesus Christ. Something which brought me closer to God happened not too long after we met in school. Mr. Bates had some heart problems and was taken to the school nurse. It just so happened that God put me in the school office at the same time, which was next to the nurse's station. Mr. Bates was in the nurse's station waiting for the ambulance to come and get him. The nurse's thought he may have had a heart attack and wanted him taken to the hospital as soon as possible. While I waited with them, I silently prayed to God to help my friend and to keep him safe. I thought of the kids and the teachers in special education who needed him. I then thought how he had brought me closer to God and how I wanted him around more. God had truly placed Mr. Bates in my path to show me how even one can bring the love of God to others just by being there. Mr. Bates is okay today and doing well in another job, but those kids and I will never forget the guitar player named Mr. Bates, who was almost never unreasonable, illogical, or self-centered.

If you are kind, people may accuse you of selfish, ulterior motives. Why are you being nice to me? What do you want? Ever hear that before or other things like, "Oh, here sits the favorite child"? "The only reason you get what you want is that they think you are nice to them." "You can't be kind to everyone; they will take advantage of you." Here come some of those stories again. Can't you remember when you were fifteen and you had to go looking for your sister? You came home without her, and he hit you hard in the head. You tried to be kind and find her, but it wasn't enough to just look for her, you had to find her and bring her home. You didn't, so you got hit in the head with his fist. You and your friend had been out for almost two days looking for her but had run out of places to look. You went back into the old neighborhoods where you had lived before to see if she went there first, but to no avail. You went back just to get knocked in the head, and it appeared no one cared. They accused you of being selfish and only wanting to run around with your friends. You weren't really out there looking for her or you would have found her. You weren't thinking of me and your mother; you only wanted to be out running around with your friends. Kindness grows on you, sometimes in very small amounts at first. Keep doing that thing they call kindness. They will eventually realize you would be kind anyway.

If you are successful, you will win some false friends and some true enemies. They all want something from you, don't they? What could it be that you have and they don't? Could it be you have succeeded where they have failed and they want what you have? Oh, you are successful, and those around you know it. That is why they are there. They want to ride on your success as far as it will carry them. Why work when he can do all of it and we take the credit? You might even see those who hate you for what you have done. They could have been just as successful if they had your opportunities. No one gave them a thing, and that's why they are not where you are. True enemies who would at a moment's notice turn you over to the lions. Success means you can share what you have with those God has put in your path. Give what you have received to others so that all will be closer to God.

If you are honest and frank, people may cheat you. It doesn't matter either way; people have a tendency to cheat you, anyway. Being honest gives you the opportunity to give without regret to those who are honest and would appreciate what you do. However, being frank to most anyone these days could get you in trouble. People don't want to know their faults and if you bring them up, it can get awkward. There is that little story in the Bible about the guy who was told to go to Nineveh. Remember, he didn't want to go and just ignored God and went the other way. He was frank with God and told him those people aren't going to listen to him, so why should he travel all that distance for nothing? That was frank, wasn't it? So what did God do to Jonah? He convinced him that going to Nineveh and telling the people was the right thing to do. You or I may not have done it the way God did, but we would have to have been frank. So Jonah went and was honest with the king, and the people repented and turn away from evil and toward God again. Sometimes it pays to be honest and frank, but choose your sentences well or ask God to help you.

What you spend years building someone could destroy overnight. Then some say that you are only one paycheck away from living in the street. God put us here to be his children and wants us to succeed. So build on your future until it's time to be with our Lord. Never stop building on what you have. It's like something I saw when I was a boy living with my dad and mom on Mississippi Street in Vallejo, California. My dad worked on that house by first painting the outside white with a green trim. Then he built a little fence in front with an arbor. He started to construct an area for a driveway where he could park his car, but stopped. I wondered why he had stopped after he had put up the frame, the gravel, and the rebar. He never put in the cement to finish the project, and I wondered when he was going to finish. Then I heard one of his friends laugh at him and say, "I told you so." See, my dad went to the landlord, we rented the place, and it really wasn't ours to do with what we wanted. I heard my dad say that, and then he related when he went to the landlord about what he had done and wanted to do. The landlord didn't really care. He said the landlord wasn't going to pay for all the improvements now or later. So now I knew why he never finished the driveway. He let someone destroy his building overnight, and when his so-called friend laughed at him too, well, I guess he lost all confidence in what he was building. As you see, there are many kinds of things you can call building. Some are physical, some mental, and again some are emotional. There is also your spiritual building. You can start with new paint and trim; this would be your starting a Bible study class, then building that fence with its arbor to show people the way into your life. Some will run to you to help, some will come to find help, and then some will come to destroy. Build it anyway, and make it the best you can so that all can see and appreciate what God has given.

If you find serenity and happiness, they may be jealous. When you see someone smile, doesn't it make you wonder what they are smiling about? Ask. Maybe it's the love of God that is making them smile. It has made me smile more than a few times. Be happy that you know God and that he loves us all, no matter what we do. I got a glimpse of that happiness he gives out to us all, if we really look for it. It came in a small little package, and when I first saw her, I was given the happiness God gives to us all. Her name is Jennifer and she was the first. She was small when I first held her in my arms, and she looked up at me. How wonderful he was for giving her to me and her mother. We were fortunate enough to have two more children after her, and all three have been gifts from God. Be happy with what you have, for God gives all you need.

The good you do today, people will often forget tomorrow. I always thought of myself as someone who tried to do good. However, I was not always good and had done many things I was not proud of. I learned from the Bible and friends that you can change what you do with the help of others and the encouragement of God. *So what is doing well,* you may ask. Let's start with the things you like to do, like helping your friends or family. Something I like to do is help someone I know without them knowing it. It could be as simple as dusting a table or washing a dish. Then again, God doesn't count the size of the gift, but the intent. Why do you want to do well? Is it for your own satisfaction or truly to help someone in need? Do you do this so that when asked you can say that it makes me feel good to do something good, because God does things for us all everyday? Do good because it helps others, some even when they don't think they need it. This winter in the middle of the Midwest, ice and snow storms caused us to have no electricity. We kept warm by using the fireplace and heating water and food from the fire. After three days, we started to run out of dry wood to burn and called a friend. He came over with a truckload of wood, and we were able to keep warm until the electricity came back on. There was never a discussion of cost for the wood, but my wife gave him a check. I didn't even ask what she gave him, nor did he say anything, either. A friend does well for a friend, a brother or sister does well for a brother or sister. God does everything for us, and he never asks what we will do in return; do good anyway.

Give the world the best you have and it may never be enough. Don't we all know those who are never satisfied? No matter what you do for them, they are never happy. If they are not the center of attention, you are not making sure they are. This brings to me something I remember as a child. I wanted someone to believe in me and acknowledge what I had done, even when I was young. Then throughout the years I would look to see if I had been acknowledged. My best friend and wife had on more occasions than I could think acknowledged my best. It still makes me happy to think of those times and the look on her face when she did. I am lucky in that I have a best friend, but alas, some don't. I for years wanted my dad to acknowledge what I had done, but it never came. Then if it did, it was always secondhand. Someone would say, "Oh, I heard your Dad say something about you just the other day." Then when I least expected it and after many years, I got the opportunity to really know what that sentence represented. I felt the presence of God next to me, and I don't know if it was in words or feelings. I knew he, God, was proud of my best and encouraged me to continue doing my best for others. So give your best, even though it may not be enough. Don't stop because you think it's not enough, for when you become weary, call on the one who stands next to you. He will give you the strength and ability to do more.

You see, in the final analysis, it is between you and God. Do what our Father wants us to do: love one another, give of ourselves to others to help, encourage, and forgive. After all, it was never between you and them, anyway. Amen.

My Wish for You

This is a song that I have heard lately and wanted to write about. The band Rascal Flatts is a country band and was recently at the Country Music Awards show. The song "My Wish For You" was brought to my attention by my daughter, who related that it made her feel good. Let's start with the beginning, which talks about making choices in your life. God allows us to make choices—some good, some not so good—but because he loves us, he allows us to choose. How would you feel, or should I say, how did you feel the first time you made a decision and carried it out? The question is, did you do it for yourself, for another person, or for the glory of God? It really doesn't matter at this point, but hopefully it has put something in your head that will click the next time you make a choice. *Am I doing this for me, for someone else, or for the glory of God?* There is another part to this as well. When it's dark and cold outside, let them see the warmth of your smile. We as Christians are to show the warmth of Jesus Christ to all who will see. It doesn't matter how bad it is for you now; God will protect you and give you what you need. So, when it's dark and cold outside, show the world the warmth of God, which shines in you.

The next part of the song has four parts. The first is that your life is all that you want it to be. The second is your dream be always big, your worries always small. The third is that you never have to carry more than you can hold. Finally, while you are working on your life, you know that someone loves you and wants for you the things you want.

What do you want your life to be? We sometimes work on what we want when we really don't know what that is. We try new things in the hope that this job will be the one you will stay with all your life. Decision making isn't as easy as you thought. Well, this again is where God comes in. Ask and you shall receive. Have you heard that someplace? In Matthew 7:7–8, it says, "Ask and it will be given to you; seek and you will find; knock and the door will be opened to you. For everyone who asks receives; he who seeks finds; and to him who knocks, the door will be opened." God is standing next to you to grant whatever you need. All you have to do is ask. Note I said need. I want a motorcycle—yeah, like that's going to happen. Sorry, but you really don't need one right now. God understands what we need better than we know ourselves. Don't you ask him to guide you through the times that are difficult for you? *God, please help me get through this crisis so that I can care for my family.* How many times do you think that prayer has been said? Go out there and with God at your side, make those decisions about life that honor you and honor God.

The next is that your dreams stay big. It's wonderful to dream. I dreamed that my backyard was a show place. Nice dream. But God wants your dreams to be big. He wants you to try all that he has provided for you here on this earth. Then he wants you to take your dreams and share them with others. At this point, my children would say, "Oh, no, he's going to tell one of his stories." He also wants your worries to be small. When they are small, you can handle them, but sometimes they are far from small. Your worries can cause you to become ill, hurt you and your family's relationships, and cause you not to trust anyone ever again. It's not to say you or we don't cause the worries ourselves, but if they start to get past a point that is uncomfortable, what do you do? I know the answer, coach. Turn to the one that waits to help you, who with a smile on his heavenly face opens his arms to you. "Give me your burdens and I will carry them for you. He's my brother and he really isn't heavy. I'll carry the burden for you, if you just ask." In Matthew 6:25–34, it says, "Therefore I tell you, do not worry about your life."

The third was that you never had to carry more than you could hold. In Matthew 11:28–30, it says, "Come to me, all you who are weary and burdened, and I will give you rest. Take my yoke upon you and learn from me, for I am gentle and humble in heart, and you will find rest for your souls. For my yoke is easy and my burden is light." If you feel the burdens of everyday life are getting to you, then turn to the one who wants to help. Our Lord and Savior Jesus Christ is there to help us ease that burden. I know how those burdens can get you down and wear you out. You don't want to do anything. You lie around your house and complain that no one is giving you a fair chance. Stop what you are doing and ask God to help. That is what he is there for. He loves us more than I could ever tell you in our lifetime. Ask him to help lighten that burden, then go out and find what you want. Don't worry about what is going to happen. Trust in God and continue to move forward with his grace.

The last part was who loves you. When your get into what you get into, just remember who loves you, too, and wants the same as you want for you. "He so loved the world that he gave his only begotten son, so that we may have life eternal" (John 3:16). That sums it up pretty much, don't you think? How can anyone even imagine how much God loves us all? I was fortunate enough to get a very small touch of that love, and it has changed me forever. I still tear up at times when I feel his presence, when I know his work is at hand and those who receive it are changed as well.

Now to another part of the song which is about forgiving those who offend you. It also reflects what you should do for those who uphold your beliefs and how you should share the love of God with all. "Who is a God like you, who pardons sin and forgives the transgression of the remnant of his inheritance?" (Micah 7:18). He forgives us, so why can't we forgive others? Let me elaborate on that forgiveness thing a little. We humans have a hard time with forgiveness from both sides. We can't imagine that God would really forgive us for what we have done. I myself have done things that would make many people shiver in place. However, I got that little glimpse of his love and really know that what I have done doesn't compare to what I can do for God. He knows that and is now using that to glorify him to others. Yet even I still have a problem with forgiving those who have done something to me I didn't like. I want to forgive them, but it seems every time I look at them, the past deeds are remembered. I will ask God for forgiveness and the strength to forgive those who I need to forgive. Besides, forgiving someone and then helping them makes them wonder how you got so close to God and they haven't. Then to the part about giving, where it is said that you receive, therefore you should give back even more than you received. It's in the Bible, and we should try our best to give to others as God wants us to. However, I really have a problem with that one, because I know how much I have been given every time I look around me. So I do what I can and give where I can. God knows what you are doing, so when you can, give all you have to anyone who needs it. Do it with grace and humility so that even the one who receives knows that the gift is from God.

In conclusion, my wish for you is in this passage: "Jesus replied; 'Love the Lord your God with all your heart and with all your soul and with all your mind. This is the first and greatest commandment. And the second is like it: Love your neighbor as yourself. All the Law and the Prophets hang on these two commandments'" (Matthew 22: 37). If you can do this, you will both honor yourself and God. Your wish for others will come true for them and for you. Thank you, Father, for the gifts you give to us everyday, and I hope my wish is your wish. Amen.

Conclusion

There will be a time when you will sit alone. No one will be around to bother you. You may never think it could happen, but it will. He will stand beside you, encouraging you to tell others of his love for them. If you have followed what has been written in the Bible, you will stand beside someone else, encouraging them and telling them about the love God has for us all. Don't be afraid; just say thanks to the Father and to the Son who stands beside you today.